The Track of the
Wild Otter

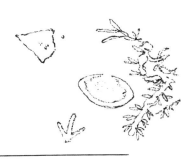

COLIN BAXTER PHOTOGRAPHY LTD · LANARK

The Track of the Wild Otter

by HUGH MILES

Drawings & paintings
by John Busby

To Bobby and Betty whose help, kindness and encouragement made both film and book possible, and whose friendship left myself and family with a host of happy memories.

The photographs on pages 26 (bottom picture), 95, 102, 126, 134, 135, 138, 139, 152 (bottom picture) and 150 are by Bobby Tulloch. All other photographs by Hugh Miles.

First published in Great Britain 1984
by Elm Tree Books/Hamish Hamilton Ltd
Garden House 57-59 Long Acre London WC2E 9JZ

First published in paperback 1989
by Colin Baxter Photography Ltd
Unit 2/3 Block 6 Caldwellside Industrial Estate
Lanark Scotland ML11 6SR

Copyright © 1989 by Hugh Miles
Drawings and paintings copyright © 1989 by John Busby

Book design and maps by Norman Reynolds

British Library Cataloguing in Publication Data

Miles, Hugh
The track of the wild otter
1. Otters
I. Title
599.74 447

ISBN 0-948661-06-2

Typeset by Servis Filmsetting Ltd Manchester
Printed in Great Britain by
John Bartholomew & Son Ltd Edinburgh

Contents

		Maps	6
		Acknowledgements	8
		Introduction	9
CHAPTER	1	The Impossible Task	11
CHAPTER	2	On the Right Tracks	23
CHAPTER	3	Failure	39
CHAPTER	4	She Trusts Me	51
CHAPTER	5	Tragedy	67
CHAPTER	6	Try, Try Again	87
CHAPTER	7	Midsummer Madness	99
CHAPTER	8	Success at Last	111
CHAPTER	9	Tracks in the snow	123
CHAPTER	10	Fishing in the Summer Sun	131
CHAPTER	11	Nostalgic Return	147
		Technical Notes	160

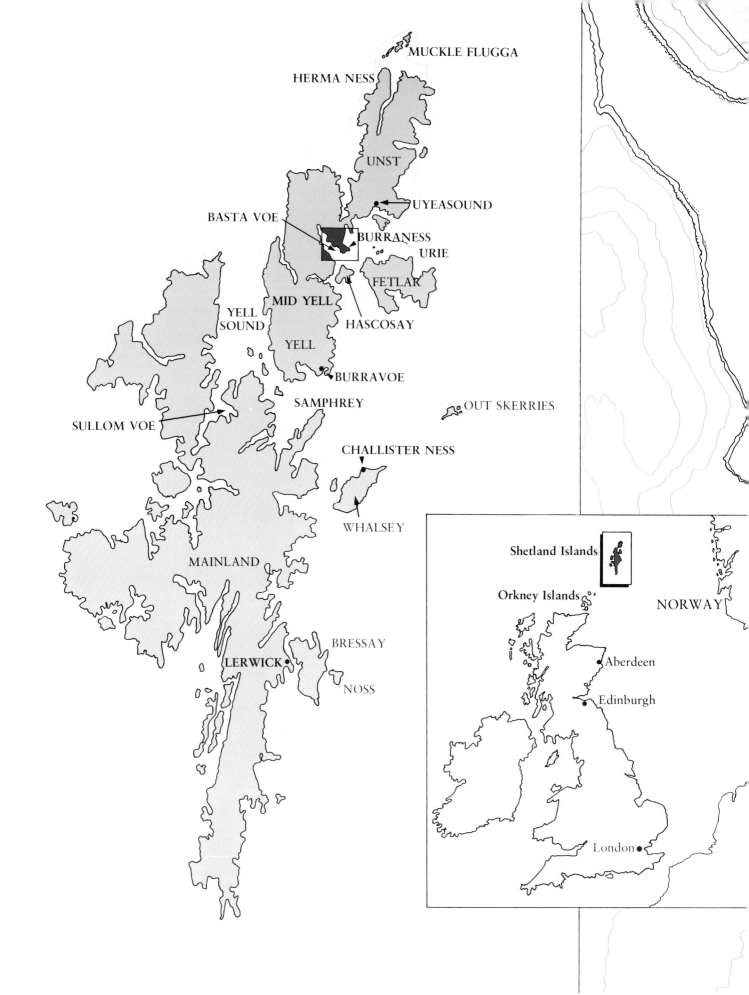

MUCKLE FLUGGA

HERMA NESS

UNST

UYEASOUND

BASTA VOE

BURRANESS

URIE

FETLAR

MID YELL

YELL
SOUND

HASCOSAY

YELL

BURRAVOE

SAMPHREY

OUT SKERRIES

SULLOM VOE

CHALLISTER NESS

WHALSEY

MAINLAND

BRESSAY

LERWICK

NOSS

Shetland Islands

Orkney Islands

NORWAY

Aberdeen

Edinburgh

London

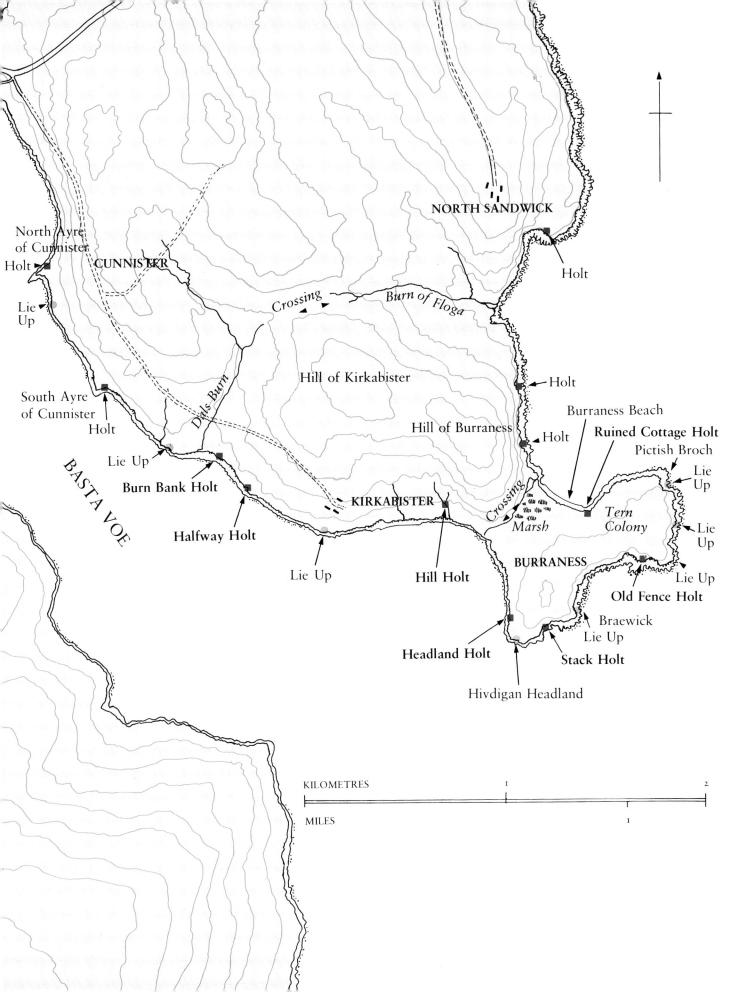

NORTH SANDWICK

Holt

North Ayre
of Cunnister

Holt

CUNNISTER

Lie
Up

Crossing   *Burn of Floga*

Holt

South Ayre
of Cunnister

Hill of Kirkabister

Holt

Holt

Lie Up

Burn Bank Holt

Hill of Burraness

Holt

Burraness Beach

Ruined Cottage Holt

Pictish Broch

Lie
Up

BASTA VOE

Dus Burn

Halfway Holt

Crossing

Marsh

*Tern
Colony*

Lie
Up

KIRKABISTER

Lie Up

Lie Up

BURRANESS

Old Fence Holt

Hill Holt

Lie Up

Braewick
Lie Up

Headland Holt

Stack Holt

Hivdigan Headland

KILOMETRES   1   2

MILES   1

Acknowledgements

THOUGH ON most occasions filming otters was a lone pursuit, it was also a team effort and without generous help from many kind friends, the project would have ended in failure.

Firstly, I wish to thank the BBC Natural History Unit, particularly Dilys Breeze, for giving me the privilege of working with those delightful otters and for encouraging me during my struggles. BBC Radio Shetland also assisted by publicising my quest and the response and warmth shown me by so many Shetlanders will live happily in my memory for ever. In particular, Bobby and Betty Tulloch opened their home and hearts to us and without their warmth and encouragement, guidance and assistance, book and films would not have been possible.

From Jim Conroy of the Institute of Terrestrial Ecology, I received much encouragement and biological assistance as both of us, in our different ways, attempted to unravel the many mysteries of the otters' lives. Caroline Taggart of Elm Tree Books was a sensitive and painstaking guide, keeping me on the 'straight and narrow' and Margaret Clark was wonderfully patient at unravelling my writing and producing the manuscript.

To John Busby I would like to extend another warm hand of thanks; we spent many happy hours with the otters and John's creative skills have done much to capture the atmosphere and thrill of those moments. It is in the hope of sharing these joys and privileges with you that Bobby, John and I have produced this book.

Introduction

FROM WHERE I write, sitting on top of a makeshift platform in the trees, I look out over muddy creeks which flow through mosquito-infested mangrove swamps. In the distance shimmer the tepid waters of the Bay of Bengal. This is Bangladesh, a far cry from the windswept shores of Shetland, where otters surf ashore on cold, grey, waves, though this too is the haunt of a species of that most charming family of animals, the otters; in this case the Asian short clawed otter. Here too otters fish between the tides, but instead of rocks and seaweed they hunt the calm creeks and tangled mangrove stems. I have not yet seen one. However, it is not the otter I have tried for two weeks to film, growing weary in the oppressive heat. These dense forests are the haunt of another hunter, the man-eating Royal Bengal tiger.

Only six weeks ago one of these tigers killed a man not two hundred yards from where I sit, and more than a dozen people have been eaten by tigers since then. All my instincts for survival are alert, and never more so than when I am stalking otters or deer along these creeks, or sitting in a hide in thick cover to film monkeys; the experience is, to say the least, distracting.

Eight days ago, on the opposite side of the creek from where I write, I was about to step ashore from our dug-out canoe when I heard the call of a tiger cub close by. As I raised my binoculars the cub's mother appeared through the dense cover not fifty yards away, walking towards us. She took three paces closer before noticing our tense gaze, then gave us a ferocious roar, followed by the fiercest stare I have ever experienced, a stare that must have been the last that many men saw before they died. The tiger's expression will remain in my memory for ever, calculated as it was to strike fear into the strongest heart. Mine missed a few beats and so desperate was one of the boatmen to get away from the tiger that he fell in the river! Honour satisfied perhaps, the tiger did not attack but walked back into the steaming jungle.

We have seen neither the mother nor her cub since then, despite a week's dawn to dusk vigil on this platform. Neither have we seen any other tigers and the beast is fast joining that most challenging category for wildlife film-makers, the 'impossible' category. The tiger has never been satisfactorily removed from this elite group of animals, and it doesn't look as if I will be the one to achieve that distinction.

Only three years ago the wild otter was also in this 'impossible' category. It was then that I was fortunate enough to be asked to attempt to make a film for the BBC series *Wildlife on One*, and subsequently *World About Us*, on this most attractive but elusive of mammals. But was it an 'impossible' assignment? Attempts had been made to film the European otter in the wild before and these had largely failed. There was no reason to suspect that I would fare any better but it was a fascinating challenge for a wildlife film-maker and I could not resist it.

Developing the will and technique to overcome the problems, and the subsequent relationship that I developed with a family of wild otters, and one otter in particular, is the story of this book.

CHAPTER 1

The impossible task

DAWN LIGHT struggles through the clouds and the hundred islands of Shetland loom up through a grey drizzle, low dark humps in a hostile ocean. The heavy sky seems full of foreboding, and I hope that my chances of filming its wild otters are not as remote as these most northerly British Isles.

Many naturalists go years without seeing an otter, and sadly it is becoming more difficult every year. Their last strongholds are now the north and west coasts of Scotland and the Outer Isles; places where otters can live and fish in peace and take a crop from the rich pickings of the sea. At least the European otter has the advantage of adaptability, being equally at home on the willow-shadowed backwaters of southern streams, or the storm-washed shores of our remotest coasts.

But why is the otter so difficult even to see, let alone film? If you described it as shy, elusive, unpredictable, nocturnal and rare and added that it lives in remote, wild places and that little is known of its habits, then you would have it in a nutshell. Such an animal is bound to be a fascinating challenge, but why it is one of Britain's most popular mammals is more difficult to fathom. Perhaps it is this very 'untouchable' quality that gives it an air of mystery and gives us such a thrill if we sight it. Man is naturally attracted to such wild, untamed animals; perhaps we have inherited a feeling of admiration for a quarry which our distant ancestors found difficult to hunt, or of which they were afraid. Many of us are excited by difficult or dangerous animals, predators such as the lion, tiger, polar bear, eagle or osprey, and other less obvious animals have 'charisma' too; the penguin, whale, owl, seal and even the lowly hedgehog. Certainly the otter has plenty of characteristics that appeal to us: its attractive looks, charming cubs, playful nature and fish hunting habits make it a delightful animal to watch. A film on such a creature was almost certain to be a success, but was it possible? Shetland probably has as many otters as anywhere in Britain, perhaps more, but the coastline stretches round the islands and skerries for more than a thousand miles; as the steamer entered Lerwick harbour in heavy rain, the task ahead of me appeared daunting.

Though I felt far from confident as I stepped ashore I was not to be alone on this assignment, for I was greeted by that doyen of Shetland naturalists and ornithologists, Bobby Tulloch. He and his wife Betty were to make me welcome at their house on the island of Yell for visit after visit, and their friendship and encouragement was to keep me going through the trying times ahead. In fact Bobby had a major hand in my being here at all. During a discussion with BBC producer Dilys Breeze, who had conceived the idea of a programme on otters, they decided that there was a chance of filming them in Shetland. Dilys had sent me north with a clear brief: 'Find out if it is possible to film detailed behaviour of otters in the wild, and don't feel too badly if you fail.'

I had an uncertain two weeks ahead of me: would I experience depressing failure, or prove that the 'impossible' wasn't? I had the best possible ally in Bobby, for in his travels as the RSPB's representative in Shetland he has probably 'met' more otters than any other naturalist alive.

Shetlanders do not see otters, they 'meet' them, a sure sign of their affection and respect for the animal and a ready acceptance that such a meeting is an event in their lives. Bobby's first encounter with an otter happened when, as a small boy, he came across a large brown 'cat' eating a fish on the rocks below his croft. To his amazement it jumped into the sea and disappeared, leaving him quite upset that it had drowned!

When economic hardship dictated that every resource be utilised the otter's pelt provided a valuable income. The old way of catching otters was by 'otter-house', a box trap built of stone on a well known 'gaet' or run; a mirror was sometimes placed opposite the entrance to excite the animals' curiosity. On entering the trap a trip-wire released a trap door over the entrance, and a large stone covered a hole in the roof through which the otter was killed and removed.

A story well-known in Shetland tells of a hunter called Robbie o' the Glen, who on finding an otter in his trap, killed it (or so he thought), pulled it out by the tail, slung it over his shoulder and made for home. The otter, which had only been stunned, suddenly came to life and grabbed Robbie by the tail! The impasse was only broken when Robbie, no doubt in agony, cried out, 'Let be for let be' and each let go his hold on the other. Although

Robbie and the otter have long since passed on, the saying still remains as the Shetland equivalent of 'Live and let live.'

Otters are now welcomed in croft outbuildings and byres where they sometimes take up residence, and with a recent law to protect them as well as the goodwill of most Shetlanders, they have less call on their wits for survival. As a result otters are slowly becoming more numerous and sightings more regular, but Bobby would be the first to admit that these are mostly chance encounters. You do not go out with the express purpose of seeing an otter!

Such was the background to our task as Bobby slipped his mooring in Mid Yell Voe on a fine morning in March, and headed out into the bay, to meet a wild otter; well, at least we could try!

Murphy's law is operating as usual; I should have been here last month! Bobby tells me that in mid-February a sub-adult otter spent several days fishing in the harbour we are just leaving; it has not, of course, been seen recently! However, the boat has hardly started to create a wake before we pass an otter's 'holt' or den, a jumble of black rocks in the back of a cave. Overhead, fulmars soar in the cliff's updraught, prospecting for future nest sites and on a ledge just above the holt a raven incubates its clutch of eggs, snuggled down out of the cold wind. Bobby has seen otters entering this holt on several occasions, but there is nothing here to excite us today. Motoring on, we check a similar holt on a nearby holm, the empty entrance washed by the swell which rolls in from the ocean.

We head out across the sound to Hascosay, a soft, low-lying isle between Yell and Fetlar. Cliffs on the southern and eastern shores are a rampart to the storms, and also provide nest sites for many seabirds. Where the cliffs are cracked there are numbers of delightful black guillemot, locally and more charmingly named 'tystie'. There are at least two otter holts in these cliffs but it is along the northern and western shores that they are most numerous, a surface of peat providing easy burrowing. With a low-lying shoreline and extensive offshore shallows, it provides everything an otter might dream of, especially as the once inhabited farmhouse now lies deserted. The wildlife of the island is disturbed just once a year, when the shepherd comes to roo the sheep of their valuable wool.

It is in the bay below this farmhouse that we quietly lower the anchor and row stealthily ashore. Just behind the pebble beach lies a small lochan, insignificant by normal standards, but not if you are an otter watcher. On his surveys of the island's bird life Bobby had on occasions seen otters here, and determined one day to photograph these elusive beasts, he set a hide in the peat bank by the shore. Armed with warm clothes, a flask of coffee, and

a bottle for a dram or two, he sat in the hide from 7 p.m. until 9 a.m. the next morning and saw absolutely nothing! He does admit to dozing off once or twice, and was woken at 2 a.m. by the high-pitched whistle of a nearby otter; but despite the bright moonlight, the whistler remained hidden.

As we search the shores of this lochan, signs of fresh otter activity are everywhere; grass worn by repeated journeys to the water, pad marks and scratches in the peat banks and holes rubbed smooth by the otter's velvety pelt. On several prominent mounds we find piles of 'spraints', fishy remnants of the otter's previous meals, vital clues for an otter tracker and equally significant to otters, for by such means they communicate their presence to each other. We walk south along the sea shore, the peat bank honeycombed by rabbits, with the occasional more extensive burrowing of an otter; each of these holts is marked with scratches and spraints. We search the rocky shore and the gently swaying beds of tangle, but if otters are present, we fail to see them.

We retrace our steps and head north past the wee lochan. Dusk

approaches, the sea is calmer now, our chances of seeing fishing otters improving. We pass another holt at the head of a small geo, a great slab of rock providing a roof for their slumbers. There is another extensive holt in the peat bank at the north west corner of the island and signs of recent use, but the occupants remain hidden; such is the lot of those who go out to meet an otter. Their presence is obvious; setting eyes on them a different proposition. As we chug back to Mid Yell in the gathering darkness we reflect that it will certainly not be the last time we will head home without seeing an otter.

❖ ❖ ❖

Next day dawns with clear skies and a calm sea, a rare treat in Shetland, where any day with much less than a gale is a fine day! We head out towards Fetlar, a fertile island to the east of Yell and Hascosay, and about an hour's boat journey away. We take advantage of the conditions to search for otters, and motor slowly up the west coast of Hascosay – but nothing disturbs the calm. The conditions are much appreciated by numerous common seals, hauled out sunbathing on a pebble beach at the north of Hascosay. I make a mental note of the location in case I should require a film sequence of sunning seals, then leave them undisturbed, heading out across the sound to Fetlar, now choppy with the last of the ebb tide.

We have decided to investigate the west coast first, for the shore just to the south of the old pier is a favourite haunt of otters. As I tie up to the pier Bobby points out a large crack in the ageing concrete out of which he once flushed an otter, evidence of their willingness to investigate any small crevice as a possible lie-up. Bobby has often seen otters here and we are full of anticipation as we walk south, keeping a careful watch on the rocks and seaweed just offshore. Several shallow pools of water in the peat above the beach show signs of extensive otter activity and Bobby knows of a holt just ahead of us; we approach cautiously. The holt consists of a large hole in the bank, guarded by two impressive lichen-covered rocks, so forming a small cave, the back of which we cannot see; the roof drips generously. By human standards it does not seem a cosy noost, but it has been used by many generations of otters, perhaps because the sloping grey slabs provide surreptitious access to the sea, only fifteen feet below the holt. It will not be an easy place to film but I work out in advance the place I will hide, just in case the otters oblige.

We walk on, finding an old spraint where a small stream crosses a beach, but the smooth curve of silver sand is untouched by the tracks of an otter. Ahead lie the Red Banks of Fetlar, nine hundred feet of loose scree, the red sandstone shale sliding steeply into the sea. I find it difficult to believe that an otter would have a holt at the top of these cliffs, but they have been seen on a number of occasions, climbing carefully up and down the slippery precipice. We decide the chances of filming such an event are slight, so we retrace our steps back to the old pier.

We have not walked half a mile when Bobby whispers excitedly, 'Otter!' and instinctively crouches down. I equally instinctively point my camera at the water but cannot see the beast; I have a lot to learn. Bobby hurriedly gives me directions and eventually I pick up the otter, heading towards the holt through the rocks and tangle, now washed by the flooding tide. The speed with which it moves fools me completely, and my lens keeps on lagging behind its lithe movement. Hardly have I started the camera than the otter is gone, and though we search for more than an hour, we cannot find it again. Perhaps it used that well worn and well hidden trail up to

the holt, and is hiding, secure, inside. However, it is a terrific thrill to have seen our quarry, even if only briefly, and we motor back to Mid Yell reasonably pleased.

✻ ✻ ✻

In a state of considerable anticipation we return to Fetlar early the next day but after a long and fruitless wait at the holt, we become restless with failure and, feeling disappointed, decide to explore further up the coast. About a mile north of the old pier is the new ferry terminal of Oddsta. The quay for the 'roll on, roll off' boats is constructed of huge granite boulders, dumped fairly loosely into the deep water, and throughout the islands these ferry terminals are used by otters, for they provide ideal holts; the quay at Oddsta is no exception, having been adopted within days of its construction. The ferrymen frequently meet otters here and last autumn saw one coming out of the ladies' loo. Not only was it very well house-trained but it could read too – it was a female otter!

Most of the north and west coast of Fetlar is favoured by otters, so we head for the ancient and now ruined village of Urie, complete with small harbour in which to hide out boat. The once thriving fishing community had their houses on a slight peninsula, and from this spot we are able to command a view over the large bays on either side. Using the ruins for cover and hours of patient scanning with binoculars we feel sure we will see any otter that is active in the area. A bitterly cold north wind occasionally forces us to retreat to the boat to warm icy hands and faces, but our vigilance does not relent. Whilst brewing coffee and making chunky cheese sandwiches we wipe the condensation from the windows and keep our eyes glued on the sea.

Our perseverance is rewarded in mid afternoon when we sight an otter fishing in the bay to the west; we hope it will come within range of the camera but sadly it remains a distant speck and eventually disappears. Encouraged by seeing an otter on two consecutive days we decide to explore the rocky reefs and small islands nearby; maybe we will find a holt that is in regular use? The area looks like a sailor's nightmare, but Bobby's years of ornithological surveys have taught him the safe channels. He has come to grief only once, and then luckily he was close enough to Fetlar to run the boat ashore before the gaping hole in the hull sank him. As we manoeuvre gently around we keep a sharp lookout for otters, whilst numerous basking seals keep a sharp watch on us. The flooding tide will soon wash them from their rocks of slumber, so we leave them in peace and land quietly on Urie Lingey, out of their sight. Climbing up to the top of the island, it becomes obvious that otters regularly tread the path we are following. The grass and sedges are smoothed by their travel, with here and there scratches or slides where they have tobogganed down the steeper stretches on their silky bellies. On top of the island are the old peat diggings of the fishermen of Urie, and in them a really large holt, or more correctly several holts, for there are many smooth burrows with large patches of spraints outside, old, and very fresh.

OPPOSITE ABOVE
. . . nothing disturbs the calm . . .

BELOW
. . . I decide to concentrate on this stretch of coast . . .

As dusk is fast approaching, and the cold of a clear March evening is beginning to bite, we decide to head for home. The evidence suggests that tomorrow we should definitely come back here to Urie.

* * *

We are blessed with yet another day of sunshine and I film a common seal basking on a rock near Urie harbour, its outline broken by darting sparkle from the back-lit sea; we scan the bay from the ruins, enjoying the unseasonal warmth ourselves. After a couple of hours I receive a shot of adrenalin which galvanises my whole body; an otter is suddenly there offshore. It seems one does not see them arrive or leave; like Merlin they just appear and disappear, as if by magic. This one is fishing near a reef some seventy yards offshore, too distant to be ideal but well worthwhile, and after a brief search in the waves my lens latches on to it. The otter is coming towards the reef, seemingly half submerged and occasionally sinking altogether. It takes a while to realise it is struggling with a very large fish, but by then it has disappeared behind the rocks.

I carefully move position, just in time to see the otter struggling to drag a fish nearly half its size on to a boulder clear of the tide. The fish is an enormous female lump sucker, with grey looks every bit as ugly as its name. It is evidently still alive, for it flaps lethargically, the otter standing on it in the style of a hunting trophy. It proceeds to eat the soft parts from the belly, causing much interest amongst the herring and great black-backed gulls, which stand close by expectantly. After a feed of a few minutes the otter slides into the water, and searches around the shallow reef for some alternative fare. It slithers between the rocks and through the seaweed, occasionally revisiting the lump sucker, either to give it a sniff or to drag it higher on to the rock, for the incoming tide is threatening to wash it away. After a few more bites of the fish the otter leaves the reef completely, swimming around the peninsula into a rising swell; though searching intently we fail to see it again.

Interested to see just how big the lump sucker is, and more importantly to take a shot of the discarded prey, Bobby rows me across to the reef. I step into the rising water and am amazed to see the fish's heart is still beating, despite the fact that a substantial portion of its soft parts have been eaten. I film the dying remains, the snow-covered crags of Stackaberg forming a background. I imagine that up there, near its famous nest site, the remaining female snowy owl is watching our antics with its piercing yellow eyes.

* * *

Encouraged by capturing our first good sequence of otter behaviour on film, we return to Urie the next day but our elation is short lived. We see absolutely nothing all day, and it rains hard in the late afternoon. Undaunted we return early the following morning, on a day of warm sunshine and hardly a breath of wind. After mooring our boat in the harbour we creep ashore and set up our stall by the ruins for a long wait. After a time I became aware of a 'presence', a sense that something is about, indefinable, but tangible enough to encourage me to creep forward towards the sea. I cast my eyes carefully over the rocks and weed and after a few minutes become aware of a ball of brown fur, moving gently with the deep breaths of sleep. I am standing on loose pebbles but have to try to move forward to get a clear shot. Each pace seems to take an age as I lower my weight on to each insecure foothold, tension in every step. The slightest rattle of a pebble will ruin a great opportunity, but eventually I have the camera set up some twenty yards from the sleeping otter. It has its back to me, but is becoming restless in the rising breeze and eventually looks over its shoulder. Much to my surprise it does not bolt into the sea, but looks at me with a myopic gaze. From its broad muzzle and whitish, whiskery features it is evidently an old and sleepy male, for he promptly curls up again, gives a deep sigh and is lost to the world.

Keen to see the effect of playing a recording of an otter cub to an adult otter, Bobby, who is some ten yeards behind, switches on his recorder. The loud squeaks of a cub ring out, but the otter does not even twitch. Thinking it is fast asleep I try to signal to Bobby to turn up the volume and do so by moving my hand no more than a couple of inches; but that is two inches too much. The otter must have been watching, for it shoots over the rocks into the sea, never to be seen again.

This reaction to such a small movement suddenly makes me acutely aware of the challenge I have set myself and I reflect on how little I have achieved. In a week I have seen otters three times and filmed two useful sequences but neither sequence is close or comprehensive, and what is more, the weather has been very kind to us. Bobby has given me lots of information on what to look for and the sorts of places Shetland otters live, but his leave has nearly run out and I can no longer rely on him to ferry me to offshore islands.

It seems sensible to concentrate on the mainland of Yell, so with further exploration in mind it is close to the remote north coast of Basta Voe that Bobby gently lowers the anchor. As he is doing so I am thrilled to see two otters together on a black outcrop of rock; I am at last beginning to get my otter-spotting eye in, for they are nearly two hundred yards away. With excitement and anticipation, we row quietly ashore in the dinghy, hiding it behind a small headland before stalking carefully towards the otters. They evidently have a fish, for two hooded crows are perched near them. The otters seem to be a courting couple, for they constantly climb back and forth on to the rocks and roll together in the water. I try to film some of this at a distance, but have hardly started before they disappear round the headland. We search hard but cannot find them again – they are like ghosts in a dream. However, a pair of otters seems an excellent omen and I immediately decide to concentrate exclusively on this stretch of coast for the rest of my stay.

I must try to learn everything I can about my chosen shore, learn to read the clues the otters leave me, to live with the tides, move silent and unseen. It is a remote, lonely spot, far from the haunts of man. I shall be on my own now, but my mood is confident; I am anxious to start. Later I lie awake, waiting impatiently for the long northern night to end.

. . . a remote, lonely spot, far from the haunts of man . . .

CHAPTER 2

On the right tracks

MARCH 20TH dawns calm, the sky dark but cloudless, a curtain of night still hanging over the sea. A touch of frost chills me as I walk slowly down the hill to my chosen shore. The turf is springy underfoot, short-cropped heather struggling through a blanket of colourful sphagnum moss, squelching from the overnight rain. Marsh grass and sedge are bent from the buffeting of south westerly gales. The grass is still now, bowed but not defeated. The sea lies below me, darkened by lingering night, the far shore of the voe a silhouette, the detail waiting to be revealed by the rising sun, hidden behind the far horizon.

There is no sound, bar the distant bleat of sheep and the murmuring of a burn that lies in the remnants of a bed of wild iris. The water chuckles down from the peaty hills, widening as it reaches the shore. The sea halts its progress here, creating a miniature estuary of mud and shingle. The stream has a name, Dals Burn, 'the burn in the dale'. Green pasture glides gently along its banks, soft light enhancing its pastel beauty.

I crouch low, not knowing where yesterday's courting otters may be hiding. I walk slowly, combing the stream banks for clues to their presence. The burn sweeps round to face the sea, and at this spot a prominent tuft has fresh spraint on it, the grass a lush green from the added nutrients. There is a patch of mud just downstream, and the pad marks of an otter; I wonder when it passed by.

To the west of the burn is a low headland, the sheep pasture sloping on to the shingle beach, its edge broken by wind and tide. I try to walk unseen, but there is no cover here; the land behind me is low. All I can do is bend double and creep along, tight against the bank. I have vowed to behave as if there is an otter round every corner, but if there is one here it remains hidden. Perhaps it watched my stealthy approach, and departed. I crouch under the bank, and scan down the coast towards the head of the voe, where land and sea merge in dawn's shadow; the shore seems lifeless.

Away to the east the sky is brighter, drawing me towards it with glimmers of hope. The tide has ebbed, exposing two reefs that jut out into the voe from the beach. I search the jumble of rock but the pools and green seaweed are punctuated only by barnacle-encrusted boulders. An oyster-catcher searches silently between them. I walk on and jump the burn, my concentration startled as a ringed plover springs up at my feet. It flies up the coast, towards the rising sun.

From the burn mouth the shore sweeps eastwards until it disappears round a rocky promontory. Several reefs jut into the shallows, and two old sheep fences march into the water in disarray, their rusty wire festooned with bladder-wrack. Of my quarry I have seen nothing, though there is now an unidentified ripple to the east; in the sunrise each little wavelet glistens silver on the calm black water.

The shoreline close to the cliff comprises shingle and black rock, interspersed with patches of washed-up weed from some previous high tide. I try to walk on solid rock, for seaweed and shingle are noisy under my heavy boots. Each step falls heavily on the silence, but leather on rock leaves no clue to my presence.

The voe is some three-quarters of a mile wide here, the land opposite a line of gentle brown hills. The peaty monopoly is relieved by a few scattered rectangular green fields, sloping down to the sea from Basta, the hamlet that gives the voe its name. On this cold calm morning the fires are lit, and smoke curls up from the three remaining inhabited crofts. A raven crosses the voe from the distant hamlet. It calls, high up in the dawn sky, and passing overhead, each wing stroke is audible as black feather beats still air. The morning seems timeless, and I imagine the day when the voe was full of ice, part of the great glacier that slithered over Shetland during the Ice Age. When the ice melted the sea level rose and flooded the valleys, creating a hundred islands, and a land where an otter can never be much further than three miles from the sea. The islands, eroded by wind and wave, provide a coastline of infinite variety and attraction to otters, and none more so than that stretching before me. Though it runs fairly straight for several hundred yards, the edge is jagged with reefs, and rocks offshore show the sea to be shallow; those revealed by the tide are festooned with seaweeds.

Behind me the coast curves back to Dals Burn and just beyond its mouth I can see the headland, and maybe any otters that swim round it. It should

be easy in the calm but a long wait here reveals nothing and I continue east. Manoeuvring round a buttress where only a narrow ledge allows me to pass, I become alert as I find evidence of the otters' passing, spraints on the edge of a slope leading up on to the moor. I follow the trail into some ancient peat diggings but fail to find any fresh signs in the labyrinth of holes in the peat. I rejoin the coast, crawling low over the edge of the cliff to avoid coming into full view of any otters that may be watching. Just ahead is the black headland on which I saw the courting otters yesterday.

An old farmhouse looms into view above the cliff and I walk up through a large bed of wild iris, once the breeding place of corncrakes. The Shetlanders who once lived here tell of being kept awake on summer nights, the twilight punctuated by the corncrakes' incessant rasping calls. The sound is akin to the rhythmic jerking of a fishing reel. The farm is deserted now, the inhabitants, like the corncrakes, long gone. The site has seen many generations of Shetlanders come and go, and there was a church here too, hence the name of the farm – 'Kirkabister'. This Christian site is a legacy of the Picts, who lived here five thousand years ago. The otters were on this coast long before them, colonising the islands at the end of the Ice Age. I search around the ruined walls of the old farm but find no sign that the otter has done the same.

I rejoin the shore down a track cut by sheep and find a hiding place behind a large rock in the edge of the cliff. It lies just above the ledge where the otters played yesterday, so I settle down for a long wait. The sun is bright now, dazzling me as I look to the east, where a great sweep of shore leads out to Hivdigan Headland. The bay it creates is calm, sheltered from the swell of wind and tide. It looks as if it would be easy to see an otter if it swam in such calm water, but the far shore is half a mile away and I begin to have doubts.

I try to become familiar with my surroundings as I wait. Lichens add colour to what at first appears a grey scene: yellow and orange on black, pastel green and white on grey, thriving in the clean sea air. I wonder at the

OVERLEAF ABOVE LEFT
. . . the stream has a name, Dals Burn . . .

BELOW LEFT
. . . the sky becomes pink with the sun's rise . . .

ABOVE RIGHT
. . . I christen this the 'Ruined Cottage Holt' . . .

BELOW RIGHT
. . . their great tower guards the bay, an ancient Pictish broch . . .

intricate, abstract patterns they make on the rocks and soak up the beauty of the scene, a vista of peat brown hills, a sky of pink and blue, distant islands shimmering across a black and silver sea. A great northern diver swims in mid-voe, close to a red-throated diver, winter visitor passing summer visitor, both lovers of northern lands. They drift slowly into the distance, to opposite ends of the voe.

I slowly become aware of the changes of pace that the shore goes through as the tide floods. To the east the common seals are washed off their hauling-out spots and as they head out into the bay to fish, they sport in the water, jumping half out and landing with a splash. To the west, three shags fish the shallows offshore. The wind rises and the splashing of wave and tide enhances the feeling of activity and anticipation. I feel that this is the moment to see an otter, but hard as I scan the shore to east and west there seems to be no sign of my elusive quarry. I become aware that I am a stranger here, unable to read the atmosphere into which I am trying to immerse myself. I feel frustrated at failing to find the otters on such a fine day for filming.

High tide approaches and the scene changes. From an atmosphere of noise and activity comes one of suspense, tangible in the sights and sounds that have dispersed. It is midday and I decide that my chances of seeing otters now are low. I can't escape the conviction that a flooding tide at dawn or dusk must be the time to see otters, so I retrace my steps along the shore, being careful as I walk, just in case I am wrong. Tomorrow I will search further afield for the elusive courting couple.

❖ ❖ ❖

I creep down to the shore at Kirkabister, having decided to start my search from where I left off yesterday. There is very little light, but a great black-backed gull leaps up into the air and moans a warning of my presence to all on the coast; I curse it silently. I feel like an intruder – there is tension in the air – I sense eyes watching my hostile form.

I head towards the first pale chink of dawn light, past the old farm, out on to the wild headland, remote from the hand of man. Several rocky promontories jut out into the bay, and I have to approach cautiously in order to check each rocky hiding place for my quarry. A small flock of turnstones twitter musically as they loop round each reef to the shingle beaches in between. A raven flies out from the hill, like a jet black kite gliding down to the shore. Two more follow, higher up, croaking deep throated calls, leaving behind some unfortunate sheep that has succumbed to the winter. A gull stands on a distant reef, looking expectant. I wonder at the significance of this and hurry towards it, jumping several boggy streams that drain the hill.

When I reach the spot the gull has gone and there is no sign of what might have been attracting its interest. I suspect a fish-eating otter and search ahead of me up the coast with renewed enthusiasm. The ground falls away into a shallow valley, then up again as the coast swings south towards the large headland. In the valley is a ditch, running north, and I am in two minds as to which way to go. I find a fresh spraint where ditch meets shore and follow what looks like an otter track in the pond weed. It follows the ditch, sometimes in the water, sometimes along the bank, even underground in places. There is a broken cobweb at one of these spots and I hurry on towards a small lochan that comes into view over the rise. Behind it is the sea, and I begin to feel sure the otter has crossed this narrow neck of land. I hurry along a sheep track which parallels the ditch, keeping watch for fresh signs of the otter's passing.

I climb the hill to get a clearer view of the lochan, flushing a curlew; it flies away, silent, pale back separating scimitar wings. No otter disturbs the dark waters of the lochan, but the scene is one of great beauty as the sky becomes pink with the sun's rise.

A small stream joins lochan with sea, crossing a majestic sweep of unsullied sand. At the far end of the beach are several ruined crofts, and sheep graze the poor pasture, just like the stock of the Picts. Their great tower guards the bay, an ancient broch, fortified against invaders. Generations of otters lived here long before it was built and no doubt they watched when the first Viking ship sailed into the bay, more than a thousand years ago.

The Vikings brought seaworthy fishing boats and were free of the Picts' dependence on hunting the shore for fish and seals; perhaps the otters enjoyed less disturbance too. They certainly survived both the Picts and Vikings and I marvel at the permanence of the animal, watching whole civilisations pass by.

The broch gives the remote headland its name, Burraness, 'the nose shaped piece of land on which stands a broch'. In the nineteenth century there were fourteen occupied houses between here and Dals Burn, providing homes for more than seventy people. Then in 1869 came the clearances. Ruthless landlords evicted the crofters to create sheep runs, and in so doing removed some of the threat of persecution and disturbance for otters. Long deserted ruins now provide the otters with shelter for their own families.

Shetlanders living today are very fond of their otters and the beautiful animals roam free on this uninhabited coast; only I continue a line of hunters started five thousand years ago. Today the otter flourishes but only thirty years ago it was still hunted for its pelt – for each one was worth a week's wages. The otter remains shy and elusive, as if remembering the threat of the human form. I must move with the stealth of a hunter, and bend low as I inspect the edges of the lochan. There are fresh spraints here, still very wet, with lots of fish bones in the pile, maybe just a few hours old. I laugh inwardly at my delight at the finding of each new pile of spraints, distasteful to some – vital to me, and the otter.

As I approach the shore, I find otter prints in the sand but they are partially obliterated by those of the gulls. Further along the beach I find more prints, following the line of high tide; this otter passed by only two hours ago. I follow the tracks along the graceful curving beach, and they lead up the beach through boulders buried deep in the sand, easy to follow despite the trickle of a stream, and disappear into a dark hole in the low bank. There is a fresh spraint at the entrance and scratch marks in the peat. Ten feet further along there is another hole, and up on the short cropped grass yet another, rubbed smooth by the otter's silky fur. It lies close to one of the derelict crofts and I christen this the 'Ruined Cottage Holt'.

To the north east is the Pictish broch, a majestic silhouette against the bright morning sky. It stands on a low hill on the far north east corner of Burraness, a fitting tribute to man's permanence against the elements. In the base of the wall is a spraint-covered ledge. I climb to the top, and find that otters have done the same, there being a highly scented lie-up amongst the fallen stones.

About half a mile further south the coast is indented by a large bay called Braewick. Within it are several flat skerries and rocky stacks and the water is shallow, for I can see the sandy patches amongst the kelp. It looks ideal otter habitat, and though I sit on the cliff top and scan for half an hour there is no sign of the otter whose tracks I had followed. I also wonder where the courting couple are? I am frustrated in my search, but can hardly complain, for sea and sky are bright, and unspoilt seascapes spread to far horizons. I feel at home in such space and walk on round the bay, looking over sheer cliffs to the crystal sea below.

. . . it seems too steep for an otter to climb up to Stack Holt . . .

The area to the south of the bay is called Hivdigan and just short of the big headland are two deep, steep-sided geos and a large stack. It seems too steep for an otter to climb the forty feet to the top, but up there are two smooth holes, with copious quantities of spraint outside. As I inspect the holt from across the yawning gap fulmars sweep effortlessly around the cliffs on taut-feathered wings, inspecting me closely with inquisitive gaze. Not surprisingly I call this 'Stack Holt', and head on round Hivdigan Headland to a holt that Bobby discovered last year.

I find the holt at the very top of the low cliff, an extensive earthwork dug deep into the peat. No doubt the wind has eroded some of the soil, but most is clearly the work of generations of otters and there are spraints old and new, scattered around outside the holt; I wonder if the courting couple are curled up snug inside. I christen this 'Headland Holt' and tread warily as I walk back towards Kirkabister, the old farmhouse clearly visible across the bay to the west. It is high water now; another six hours have passed without my sighting an otter and I limp home a little low in spirits. Even if I have found fresh tracks and discovered three of their holts, I wonder how I can break the deadlock.

* * *

Layers of pale cloud greet us as we walk over the close-cropped turf towards the shore. Bobby is with me today, most welcome company after

. . . Headland Holt – I wonder if the courting couple are curled up snug inside . . .

two days of lonely failure. As we reach my hiding place below the farm a patch of sunlight illuminates a distant island – it flows green amongst the greys of these rugged shores and seems to strike a note of optimism – it is the most perfect morning. Frost glistens on the blades of grass on the top of the cliff above us, the sea a flat calm, from one wild shore to all others. Reflections of pastel pink, blue and grey stretch far over the peaceful voe.

We don't wait long before this mirror of the dawn sky is bent by a movement to the east. An otter is swimming towards us round the headland, distant still, but its wake catches the early morning sun and flows behind it – bars of silver on a coal black sea. Progress towards us is punctuated by dives for fish, the reflections of forward motion transformed into concentric rings which spread out and slowly disappear. We crouch lower as it closes to within fifty yards of our hiding place. We think it is a female – not broad enough in the muzzle or large enough in the ear to be a dog otter. She lies on the surface for a few moments between dives, then just as she kicks powerfully with her hind legs and jack-knifes over, takes a deep breath, quite audible in the stillness of dawn. The curl of her powerful tail follows her into the depths, but the last evidence of her presence above the surface are the ever widening rings, and a cluster of bubbles which dissolve into the cold air.

We time her dives, which average twenty to twenty-five seconds, and by moving only when she is submerged we follow her along the shore. She works her way towards the west at quite a speed, and we have to run over the rocks, keeping close to the cliff to ensure she can't see our silhouettes. She seems to catch fish with ease, for every few dives she surfaces with what looks like butterfish, thin eel-like butter-coloured fish of six inches to a foot long. She treads water as she chomps them offshore, the crunching of her sharp teeth on flesh and bone quite audible above the snorting of common seals and the wailing of red-throated divers. Inexplicably, she suddenly disappears, and a careful search to east and west reveals nothing. We decide to retrace our steps, returning to our hiding place on the point.

Two hours pass before we notice a line of bubbles heading straight towards the rocks just below us. We wait tensely, peering over the rock, then suddenly a whiskery face appears between boulders at the water's edge. It looks like the female we saw earlier in the day. She stares into our eyes, gives two snorts of disapproval and plunges back into the sea. The line of bubbles escaping from her coat lead offshore, but hard as we look we fail to see her surface. We suspect she has headed west, so search the sea edge cautiously, hardly daring to move at first in case she is watching. For an hour we hunt for clues of her presence but without success, and we reflect on the remarkable ability otters have to disappear rapidly.

With wind and cloud building up, and the tide now lapping the base of the cliff, the best of the day seems to have gone and with otter-spotting difficult in the grey light and choppy sea, we head for home. Within an hour it is blowing hard from the south east, and rain rattles the window panes as we look out into the gathering darkness.

* * *

It is two days before the rain relents and sunshine breaks through the scudding clouds. The wind has swung round to the north west and freshened to a full gale, gusting storm force nine. The effect on the landscape is impressive. Grass lies flattened against the ground, sand blows off the dunes in long erratic lines. The sea is whipped into a foam which is driven inland, blowing on to the rocks below the cliff. In the bay, huge walls of green water rear up from the sound, cascading over as if in slow motion, creating a turmoil of white spray. Behind lies the mainland coast and the snow covered peak of Ronas Hill, occasionally hidden by spume. Defying the elements, numerous kittiwakes deftly collect displaced plankton from between the waves, seemingly oblivious of the water that threatens to swamp them from above. The waves turn blue with the sky, the kittiwakes grow whiter, their cries rising above the roar of wind and wave. I search this gale-blown chaos with little optimism; I can seldom find otters even when conditions are ideal – what chance now when binoculars are constantly smothered in sea spray and eyes water in the cold wind? The sunshine is shortlived and I retrace my steps in gathering gloom. Another day's rain follows.

✻ ✻ ✻

The wind dies to a whisper in the night. I awake often, restless for success, and rise before daylight in a gesture of optimism. Breakfasted, and flask of coffee prepared, I drive on round the head of Mid Yell Voe on the way north to Basta Voe. The sky is on fire as it glows from under night's towering black clouds. The voe is flat calm and I stop on the hill to check out those spots where the sky's mirror is broken. There are several ripples, a pair of eider ducks feeding, fulmars squabbling, three tystie preening, a herring gull trying to reach a sea urchin in the shallows; all is much as it should be. Then a more purposeful movement heads out from the shore. It is very distant, but obviously an otter, for it fishes the last of the ebbing tide, the ripples of its dives turned red by the rising sun. I wonder whether to walk down the hill to the shore, but the coast looks difficult for otter stalking, rising up steeply from the voe, with few hiding places. Reluctantly I decide to have yet another try for the courting couple.

I start my search from below Kirkabister once again and immediately notice a change in the atmosphere; my presence is no longer a surprise here. Walking these shores day after day I have become immersed in the scene. Gulls no longer jump up in alarm, curlews merely look up and continue to feed, rabbits just watch me pass by. It gives me a feeling of warmth to be accepted by these wild creatures and I settle into my hiding place to enjoy this new found freedom. I imagine the otter must be very sensitive to this atmosphere of peace and I am pleased that I too am learning to feel the pulse of the shore, becoming a natural part of this beautiful wilderness.

The haunting wails of red-throated divers float across the water from far out in the voe. It is quiet today, perfectly calm, but there is life along the

shore, the legacy of the gale still present, hidden power below the water causing the beds of kelp to writhe mysteriously. Only occasional fronds move, animal-like in their erratic surfacing. Rocks peep above surface, then as the swell rolls in again, disappear, causing otter-like rings to ripple out over the calm. I am kept in a constant state of alertness; it is as if the shore is torturing me, playing on my imagination in order to drive me off.

It is low water, the moon is full, the tides large. Beds of tangle and jagged reefs stretch far out into the voe. Searching will be difficult but at least I am familiar enough with the shore to be able to move along noiselessly.

Checking the burn mouth I discover a spraint so fresh it still has bubbles on it. The otter must have been here only minutes before so I bend double in an attempt to gain the cover of the peat banks without being seen. Within moments I am hidden and immediately see an otter, heading away from me to the east. It is a long way off, but it starts to fish off the red garnet headland and I move towards it as fast as I dare. Each time it dives I rush forward and am within one hundred yards when it fails to reappear. The light is difficult, the bright morning sun turning weed and rock into black silhouette, the sea a dazzling white. Of the otter I can see nothing, but I press on cautiously in the hope that I will catch up without alarming it. I am well beyond Kirkabister before I reluctantly admit that it has given me the slip.

I walk as far as the Headland Holt to see if that yields any clues but the spraints are old and a cobweb hangs over the main entrance. Retracing my steps to Kirkabister I wait for an hour for the tide to start flooding, then stalk carefully back towards Dals Burn. Just as I reach the next rocky promontory I spot an otter rolling in the tangle at the edge of the tide. I carefully move a little closer and am some four hundred yards away when a second otter's head appears close to the first. The elation at refinding the courting pair is tempered by practical considerations, for I am upwind. Darting quickly back round the promontory I return to Kirkabister, climb the sheep track, take a long sweep inland at a run, then slowly approach the edge of the low cliff on my hands and knees, half pushing and half pulling the camera. I hope I will be slightly downwind of where I guess them to be, if they are still there.

The edge of the cliff is lined with wind-blown marsh grass and I peer through this to the sea. As I rise slowly, more and more of the shore becomes visible and then I see them just twenty-five yards below me, grooming close to each other in the bladder wrack. They are certainly a pair, for the male is slightly larger, has a darker coat, broader muzzle, larger ears. The female is the same as that I have seen on previous occasions, recognisable by the distinctive spots on her top lip, that on the left of her nose being larger than that on her right. As she scratches under her chin with head raised, I notice she has only the slightest pale mark on her chest. Many Shetland otters have a distinctively shaped patch here, an aid to identification, but all she has is a small oval patch. I see the male has no mark at all, but his dark brown features and almost black face should be distinctive enough.

He rolls on his back, rubbing his fur on the wet weed in snake-like fashion, stubby legs waving in the air. The female takes this as an invitation and rushes across a rock pool, jumping on him and trying to bite him around the mouth. They whicker and squeal as they wrestle, then suddenly the female breaks off and plunges into the sea, followed closely by the male. I fear they have caught my scent, but they surface just offshore, roll close together and make several shallow twisting dives in unison, a languid water ballet of great beauty. The female surfaces slightly apart and he swims directly towards her nose, whereupon she raises a paw out of the water and ducks him playfully. After a couple of minutes of this cavorting, the female heads for shore and lands in the weed-covered shallows. He follows and sniffs closely at her behind but she swivels round in obvious aggravation and snaps at him, whickering in annoyance. The pair separate a little, and the male drinks from a rock pool, not lapping like a cat, but ducking his mouth in and throwing his head back to swallow. They groom a little more, then slide gracefully into the flooding tide. They head towards Kirkabister, swimming at some speed as they make a succession of shallow dives in line astern, serpent-like echoes of the Loch Ness monster.

I run inland, then east, jumping the marshy streams and boggy patches without slowing my stride. I slither down the sheep track and rush to my hiding place, breathless, but just in time. The pair are approaching the headland and become nervous as they approach the rocks, looking back down the coast with necks craned above the water, then sinking out of sight. Only bubbles betray their presence under the reef, but eventually the female's head appears round a rock, and she climbs cautiously ashore. She selects a flattish area which is washed by the tide and circles a couple of times before settling, curling herself up and resting her chin on her tail. The male is far more cautious and spends quite some time surfacing and submerging in the reef, looking nervously around. Several times he seems to stare straight at me but I do not move and eventually he climbs out by the female. The space between the rocks is cramped, and failing to get comfortable he decides to lie on top of the female, who resists. Whether by chance or design he places a large webbed foot on her head which effectively pins her down, and both sleep fitfully.

The tide is flowing fast now, and the female becomes almost submerged. She tries to crawl out from under the male but without success and he remains dry and asleep; she lies there, wide awake, with water lapping her face. Eventually he starts to get splashed by the waves and becomes restless himself, releasing the female, who slides away into the water. He is startled by this and follows nervously, disappearing round the back of the rock. For a time the female rests in the flooded rock pool, eyes closed, sleeping perhaps, but eventually she slithers over a shallow reef and disappears too. I search up and down the coast without success and

assume they are sleeping off the high tide in some undiscovered holt.

It is mid afternoon, the sky still bright, the wind still light. I explore the shore, trying to familiarise myself with the terrain, hoping to find other otters. I head out to Burraness again, alternating my attention between the big bay of Braewick and the Stack Holt. Nothing stirs, bar soaring fulmars along the dark cliffs, and curlews on the yellow moorland behind me. The water is ebbing now, exposing reef and tangle with surreptitious speed; the light begins to fall with the tide. There is a mysterious stillness as night approaches, the world holding its breath in anticipation of darkness.

I head back round Hivdigan Headland, still lit by the western sky. To the north, sea and shore are dark, but a ripple near Burraness ditch catches the sky's light and I hurry round in anticipation. A second ripple follows the first along the edge of the rocks towards me; the courting couple are out again. They roll gracefully together in the tangle's edge, and whilst preoccupied with each other, I rush forward and set up just above a group of prominent rocks. They head towards me, and as hoped, they approach the rocks, cautious as they leave the safety of the sea. The male checks the air for hostile scent, the female looks around briefly, then both settle slightly apart to groom. The female soon tires of this and climbs on top of the male, biting his ears playfully and attempting to chew his bottom jaw; both squeal and whicker in apparent mutual enjoyment, the male escaping her jaws by wriggling below her, but the female, still lying on top of him, re-engaging him in the play. There seems to be a reversal of traditional roles in otter courtship, the female continually encouraging the male. After several minutes of this behaviour the male lowers his chin on to the rock on which he lies, closes his eyes, and goes to sleep. The female lays her head on top of his, and somewhat reluctantly it seems, also goes to sleep. I withdraw quietly, my retreat masked by the fading light. Dusk has fallen. Darkness follows quickly from the east.

Tomorrow is April 1st and I must head south on another assignment. Reluctantly I turn my back on the shore, leaving the otters sleeping soundly, at peace with their world.

CHAPTER 3

Failure

CLOUDS CREEP after me but the skies look more promising ahead and a shaft of sun turns grey sea to silver. A distant otter swims into shadow, created by the cliff; in high spirits I walk on. A great cloud climbs the sky to the east and obliterates the sun; I shiver in the north wind and increase my pace. Living close to the weather makes me happy, walking under the shifting sun, in a world of wind and cloud, with the tide as timekeeper.

I pass below the cliff but the otter is gone. The rocks where otters courted just two weeks ago are deserted, likewise the ledge they slept on below Kirkabister. The coast seems empty without them.

I head out on to Burraness, full of anticipation, but the sprainting places are relatively unused, and what few prints there are on the sand have nearly been obliterated by wind and tide. The Ruined Cottage Holt shows little sign of occupation. I reach the broch at 7 a.m. and have a breakfast of black coffee and biscuit. I sit on a high perch against the lichen-crusted wall, just as my ancestors must have done, and there is comfort in the fact that the scene has changed little since then, despite centuries of time and tide. I am grateful for my presence here.

A sleet shower sweeps across the sound from the north, not so unseasonal for a mid-April day in Shetland. The slanting grey tower of cloud leaves Unst glistening in sunshine and the sea below me hammered smooth by the drops of ice. I turn my back on the downpour and walk south, finding it difficult to imagine the swallows I was watching in Dorset only two days ago, hawking insects over buttercup meadows. There will be other migrants hastening across hot African savannahs, driven on by the urge to find some cosy nook on these most northerly isles; it strikes me as an optimistic gesture on this wintry day.

Reaching the Stack Holt, I find the entrances smoothed by frequent use, fresh spraints on rocks, the grass trampled, a route up the cliff just discernible due to mud on stone. The decision to stay and watch is easily made and I settle down against a peat bank, sheltered slightly from the wind. But as the hours tick by and nothing stirs, I begin to doubt the wisdom of the wait. Is the otter active elsewhere, at the beach, by the broch, round the headland, back at Kirkabister? Once these nagging doubts start to gnaw away at my confidence it is difficult to wait, but difficult to know when to move, and where. Eventually I walk on round Hivdigan Headland towards Kirkabister but hurriedly, for fear of changing my mind.

There are only some three day old spraints at the Headland Holt; they are dryish and black, but a very fresh spraint at the ditch crossing alerts me to more possibilities. Has the otter swum on down to Kirkabister? Did it swim towards Hivdigan Headland, see me approaching and hide, or has it headed north up the ditch? I decide on a quick dash up the ditch to the beach; there at least the sand will give me accurate evidence if the otter has passed by.

Creeping round the lochan I discover fresh prints at the stream edge. The tracks lead down the beach and stop just two feet short of the sea. The tide is ebbing; I have only missed my quarry by a few minutes. I dare not move, only search anxiously with my eyes. The otter is here, but unseen – hidden – watching me perhaps from some weedy hiding place. A strange feeling, being watched but not knowing by whom or from where, a tightening of the nerves in neck and back, literally hair-raising, the primitive natural instincts vital to man when he was closer to animals – a hunter, and hunted. I am exposed on the open shore, vulnerable, uneasy. I retreat up the beach to cover.

Failing to discover my tormenter close by, I come out of hiding and head on round Burraness, hoping to catch up with my shadow. So goes another day, round and round the shore, drawn on by tantalising clues, distant views, decisions and doubts.

I am approaching the broch for the third time, just twelve hours after my breakfast there, when a fulmar suddenly springs up from the turf at the cliff edge and an otter appears, running, hump-backed, up the hill to the broch. It hesitates briefly to smell the scent of my tracks, then follows my path round the side of the broch and out of sight. I creep up round the other side, then see it, distant now, moving effortlessly away from me over the rocks, slipping into the sea, round the cliff into evening shadows.

The pale sun has no warmth as it slides shyly across the sea. The sky is bright still, but no longer blue – sea and sky grow grey. The light fades quickly in the western sky. By the time I reach Dals Burn night has closed around me.

* * *

I am on the shore again at dawn, but there are so few signs of otter activity that I begin to doubt their presence. Reason tells me they are still here, but the reality is less convincing. I meet Gibby soon after dawn as he walks the coast, checking his sheep and new born lambs. His wind-burnt complexion and tousled hair are ample evidence of the hours he spends on this exposed coast. We talk sheep and weather and otters. The last otter he saw was a week ago below Kirkabister, but he has not seen one with cubs for several months. His collie noses around on the shore below us. When asked if the dog worries the otters Gibby tells me the last time they came face to face the otter stood its ground, bearing its carnivorous teeth and whickering loudly, before plunging into the ocean. He imagines that in a fight the dog would come off worse. We go our separate ways, our calls of good wishes blowing away in the wind.

* * *

I spend the day hidden in a canvas hide just south of the old pier at Broch Lodge. There is a chance I will see the cubs, but all I watch is sea-birds, and a shag fishing just offshore. A bonxie flies past the hide, then suddenly hesitates in mid-air and plunges on to the shag just as it is surfacing. The bonxie stands astride its back, and holding it by the scruff of the neck, proceeds to drown it. The shag resents this treatment and puts up quite a struggle, continually raising its head above the water before having it

OVERLEAF ABOVE LEFT
. . . a great cloud climbs the sky to the east . . .

BELOW LEFT
. . . watching me perhaps from some weedy hiding place . . .

RIGHT
. . . I see an otter walking on the rocks near the sprainting stone . . .

ducked under again. Eventually, its resistance grows weak. Wind and tide carry the combatants up the coast.

✽ ✽ ✽

Determined to film an otter entering or leaving a holt, with or without cubs, I am out on Burraness by sunrise. Of the three holts I know, the only really active one seems to be Stack Holt, so I settle here, resolved to wait a week if I have to. It is in an ideal situation, the only entrances I know of facing the shore, and the otters' only approaches to it being visible from my hiding place. I sit all day in a peat hollow, watching the fulmars cackling at each other on the cliff top, beaks dripping from the intensity of their courtship. A shag dries its wings on a reef at the base of the stack, feathers held wide in the sunshine, striking a heraldic pose as the sea sparkles behind its black silhouette. The time for courtship is approaching: its crest is well formed, the wind curving it back over its emerald green eyes. Spring squill and sea pink occur sparsely, surviving only where the gnawing teeth of rabbits cannot reach. They add foreign colour to a vista of grey, green and blue, I walk home at dusk, my quarry undetected.

✽ ✽ ✽

The wind changes to south easterly overnight and I catch the full force of it in my hiding place. Huge black clouds tower up over Fetlar and the occasional shower slashes hurriedly across the sound. Cold and wet, I decide to build a hide, and amuse myself collecting driftwood and constructing a makeshift shelter. My watchfulness never slackens; it would be just like an otter to leave the holt the moment my back is turned. The old wood smells strongly of salt and weed, but, snug inside, I guess it will mask my human scent. I write a few notes, a letter or two, think, question, reason, watch and listen; the hours tick by.

My little world rolls slowly round the sun. Patterns on the sea change frequently, shafts of light pierce the threatening clouds, bars of silver glisten on far horizons, low islands shimmer in the haze. I watch the tide flow one way, then the other, musing on which other distant lands the water might have passed by. So another day drifts on, filling my head with wind and sun. There is a sense of space, peace, tranquillity, days free of intrusion from man, the feeling of isolation intensified by distant farmhouses and fishing boats returning home. Sunset fills the deepening blues with holy rays. Fulmars pass into the shadow of the cliff, filling the silence with a rush of air. Their cackled greeting rises up from the darkness below. As the great hush of night falls, the cold descends.

✽ ✽ ✽

The sun lights the sky with solar fire, I am optimistic again. Why so optimistic at dawn yet so pessimistic by early afternoon? Perhaps there is no reason to anticipate failure at the start of the day. As the hours pass by, the nagging doubts become reality. By mid-afternoon there is sadness at the loss of yet another day, gone forever. Pessimism bites deep, but evening brings with it new hope, rekindling the fires of optimism. By now it is too late for success, so the fear of failure is removed. I can enjoy dusk, for there is always the expectation of tomorrow.

❊ ❊ ❊

The tomorrows come and go. I wonder how often in these days of frustration, when I have not seen a single otter, how many have seen me and watched me pass. On my last day I walk back and forth between Dals Burn and Kirkabister, having given up hope of activity at Stack Holt. Waiting for an otter to come to me did not seem to work, so I am mobile again, pacing the shore uneasily.

At midday when some way short of Kirkabister I see an otter walking on the rocks near the sprainting stone. I circle round across the pasture, and creep quietly down the sheep track on to the beach. I stand there for a moment, deciding which way to approach the otter I believe to be just below me. That rattle on the sheep track three yards behind me must be a loose stone I dislodged, or a sheep; I hardly bother to look round, but when I do I am shocked; it is the otter, the courting female, the one I have been searching for these last ten days. She climbs carefully and unhurriedly down the track, just as I had done moments before, and walks across the beach towards me, seemingly oblivious of my presence. I dare not move, let alone swing the camera on to her, and she walks past only a yard away. She ignores me as if this is the final affirmation of her superiority. She unhurriedly slides into the water and swims away up the coast. I accept her victory and return to Dorset a failure.

❊ ❊ ❊

Sue, Katie and Peter travel north with me. It is late July, so school holidays can be enjoyed together; my children love these wild coasts. We are no sooner off the ferry from Aberdeen than on to another, to the island of Whalsay. We have been informed of an otter cub sighting here, courtesy of BBC Radio Shetland, who kindly keep the islanders informed of our requirements and progress. I leave Sue and the children to amuse themselves on a remote beach near the north west corner. The day is rather grey, clouds threaten rain; not an ideal day for the beach, or otter filming, but the occasional burst of sunshine keeps my spirits up, and I hope those of my family.

I head away from them to the west; it was just round the far headland, during a sheep drive, that the otter cub was sighted. I disturb a female eider with two small chicks, the mother drab brown, the chicks a fluffy buoyant black. They head offshore into a deep swell, appearing and disappearing in unison; I move on quickly so they can regain the safety of the rock pools. Only two survivors from a brood of perhaps ten bear witness to the poor summer weather Shetland has suffered.

I reach Challister, Ness and search the area for holts and clues to the

otter's presence. The shore is rugged now, the cliffs high, with huge caves and geos carved out by the storms. In places where the elements have succeeded, huge slabs of loosened stone create dark, angular caves. I scramble about these precipitous ledges, finding plenty of evidence that the otters have done the same, but not recently. I gaze down the vertical chasms into the deep water below, and imagine the wrasse sucking limpets amongst the kelp, and the otter plunging after them. Of my quarry I see nothing.

Further south the coast becomes non-descript; short cropped pasture changes gently to rock, which in turn slides gently into the sea. I discover an otter holt on the hill, an enlarged rabbit burrow. Outside it are the dismembered wings of six storm petrels, nocturnal visitors to the islands. The only sound is the distant bleat of sheep; the only movement that of the tide slipping slyly away. My pessimism is jolted by the unmistakable squeak of an otter cub, high pitched, repetitive, piercing, monotonous; sometimes described as a short sibilant whistle, but music to my tense ears. The sound appears to come from a slight crevice in the rock to the south, so I manoeuvre round to get the light in my favour and wait with anticipation for the cubs' appearance. The next two hours are punctuated by the occasional squeak which keeps me rooted to the spot, but frustrated, for I see nothing. I search up and down the coast for the mother, in vain. Eventually the calls cease and I creep forward to investigate. The crevice is hardly big enough to call a holt, but it smells strongly of otter; I peer into the dark gloom, hoping to see a whiskery face peering through the darkness, but the cave is empty; they have given me the slip again. Both otter and time have beaten me.

✲ ✲ ✲

I am out again at 4.30 a.m. It is hardly light and gets even darker as I approach the shore; a deluge soaks me for my troubles. I am tempted to return to the warmth of my bed but these are the hours of optimism so I shrug the water off and start the long search once again. The sunrise pierces shafts of white light through the cloud in the south east, there are more showers and the breeze freshens to a gale, but the light is beautiful at times, so clear and bright, bathing the fields of dandelions in false warmth.

The marshes are filled with bog cotton, their delicate white heads nodding incessantly in the gale. Terns scream overhead, intent on feeding their young, redshank run the beaches, gannets plunge for fish far out in the bay; it is a fresh, vibrant day.

I hear the otter cub again in mid-morning, the calls blowing up to me in the gale. I rush towards the spot, an isolated group of rocks on a beach. Surely I shall see mother and cub this time, but when I reach the spot they are gone. I find their pad marks in the sand, glistening fresh. These animals are ghost-like, ephemeral, intangible, untouchable – exasperating! I expect the pad marks to fade before my eyes and they do, evaporating slowly in the wet sand. The rising tide washes the remnants away and I return to Yell.

✳ ✳ ✳

Friday 25th July is an awful day of the dullest rain and strong south east wind. Cloud hangs over the islands all day, blanketing activity in an all pervading wetness. A report of two otter cubs on the south coast of Samphrey lifts the gloom, and I head out to this small island in Yell Sound early on Saturday morning. Despite telling myself I have little chance, I feel confident and though it is raining slightly amidst the thick fog, the forecast is good. There is no sign of land in the gloom. The boat slides sideways across the current and the compass needle in Willie John's boat swings wildly in the tide rip. It's almost a surprise when the island eventually looms up in the mist, low-lying, green, rocky shored, so silent; the clatter of the anchor shatters the peace and I imagine every otter taking cover for a week but once ashore and alone, I become immersed again in the fog and the boat engine fades away.

So dense is the fog that I've no chance of seeing the otters, but they cannot see me; I shall sit near the spot the two cubs were seen and just listen. The murmur of tide through tangle and the distant bleat of sheep

merge into the background. The ear becomes attuned to more specific noises, the breaths of a porpoise, the wails of a seal, the shrill piping of an oystercatcher. A curlew flies overhead, its clear, fluting call echoed by another on some invisible part of the island. I explore up the west coast, finding numerous holts in the peat bank; many appear deserted. I walk about a mile before reaching the north end where a lochan created by two beaches virtually cuts off the headland. This is perfect otter country, but there are no fresh signs of activity. I retrace my steps to the south, anxious not to leave the area of the otter cubs too long. The sun burns off the fog and I see the island for the first time, roughly triangular in shape, flat-topped, featureless. I walk towards the sun and sit at the place of the cubs.

It is low water now, the tide is stilled, hardly a ripple stirs the shore. A herring gull lands on a nearby reef, its wing beats noisy on the silent air. It takes off when it notices me and flies round above, moaning a warning at this strange presence. I retreat and search the east coast, but this is also deserted.

I wonder at this lack of otters. Perhaps the disastrous oiling caused by the Esso Bernicia accident just a year and a half ago took its toll more seriously than suggested. Sullom Voe is only five miles across the sea from here and the oil had dire consequences for the birds in Yell Sound. 3,700 bodies were collected and it is calculated that 75% of those birds wintering in Yell Sound died. Fourteen otter corpses were picked up and a further eighteen were seen oiled, but alive. I wonder how many just slunk back home to a peaty grave.

I return down the west side, circumnavigating the island, but to no avail. The cubs will not show themselves to me, not today – I begin to believe not any day. As the miles of walking unfurl, and headland after headland reveals nothing, that familiar sense of disappointment gives way to a feeling of failure – the sensation is similar to feeling physically sick.

At 3 o'clock, after ten hours of this self-imposed torture, an otter decides to turn the screws once more by appearing close to the south eastern corner. Though weary with failure, I run the half mile to the point, just in time to see the otter climb out of the water to make a short cut over the rocks, I close in – the otter has gone, or maybe it was a figment of my imagination? I climb round the rock and there is its fresh spraint, even wet footprints on rock, it was not a dream. I lie down and shut my eyes in despair.

✻ ✻ ✻

I have one more string to my bow. Bobby's sister has reported otter cubs outside her house on the shore at Burravoe, so dawn the next day sees me walking another strange coastline. The weather is perfect but the coast is not, the moorland sloping steeply down to the cliffs, the cliffs curved convex to the sea. There are several deep geos and numerous angled jumbles of rock. It all means there are plenty of places for the otter to hide but none for me. However, I find the holt as instructed, a cave in some boulders at the head of a gully, and prepare to sit it out.

It is a calm, clear morning, the peace punctuated by the splash of the gannets' crash dive, the sound carrying far over the sea, echoing off the cliffs below. The harsh fishing calls suddenly change to ones of alarm as a piratical bonxie attempts to steal their meal. Flying amongst them, it speedily catches one up, grabs it by the tail, and tips it up, causing it to crash. Gannet and regurgitated meal end up in the sea, the bonxie collecting the easy pickings. It then goes after another, flying above the gannet and stamping on its back, an equally effective technique. Below them, a school of porpoises laze their unhurried way south, breathing in the chill air of dawn and blowing out warm spray into the breeze.

The day slips by with nothing to raise my hopes when suddenly I hear a squeaking below me and two furry brown bundles appear out of a crack. No sooner have I swung the camera on them than they are gone, but I have them marked now and adjust my position to get a better view. It is not easy on this shore and I am still manoeuvering when two ladies and a dog appear over a rise. It is a fine Sunday afternoon, perfect for a walk along the shore, but why now? An hour either side would not have mattered perhaps, but just at the precise moment when I have seen my first cubs; that is cruel luck. The dog is excited and barks loudly – I see the last of my chances evaporating away. I try to make brief, polite conversation but the words stick in my throat.

I wait two further hours and not surprisingly nothing stirs. I return home disappointed once again, wondering why I deserved such rough handling from he who dishes out the good and the bad. It rains hard for the next two days and my prospects of success seem cheerless.

✻ ✻ ✻

The sky is brighter, visibility is clear, the wind light. It should be a good day for filming the sea-birds at Hermaness, and we head north in Bobby's boat for the most northerly point in Britain. The colony is a wonderful sight, cliffs towering above us, absolutely smothered with birds, raucous calls drowning the noise of engine and sea swell alike. Showers of auks fan out from their ledges and burrows, gannets wheel gracefully above. Offshore the gannets and fulmars have discovered a shoal of sandeel, forced up to the surface by mackerel. Whilst I film their spectacular plunge dives, Bobby feathers for the mackerel, bringing them up in strings; there will be a surfeit of fish for supper tonight.

The gannets plunge so close to the boat we can see them swimming downwards below us. They use powerful beats of the wings and appear to go down twenty or thirty feet, then when their prey is captured they burst to the surface in a flurry of spray. The fish is swallowed quickly, for fulmars cackle around with excitement and the air is full of bonxies dive-bombing into the mêlée to try to steal their share. Lines of gannets heading home with bellies full of food are also strafed by the bonxies. Many get through but some are upturned by a pull of tail or wing-tip. It is a heady day of spectacle and action, fresh air and fun, a real tonic for a weary and defeated otter watcher.

Thus refreshed and invigorated, I try to devise a plan that will solve the problem of filming the natural behaviour of an otter with her cubs. I have read and admired J. A. Baker's haunting book on the peregrine in which a man, by dint of following a particular bird around, day in day out, broke down the fear of that bird. If it could be achieved with one of the wildest birds I assume it could be achieved with one of the wildest mammals. I will wear the same clothes every day, carry the same equipment, move in the same way. I have already become slightly familiar with the shore from Dals Burn to Burraness and made acquaintance with a female otter below Kirkabister a few times. I can recognise her now, perhaps one day she will learn to recognise me.

CHAPTER 4

She trusts me

AFTER WEEKS of failure on strange shores it is a relief to return to Basta Voe. I am at home here, familiar with my surroundings, confident that access and mobility are possible without showing my silhouette on the skyline. I have dyed my tripod, camouflaged the camera. I wear dull green trousers and a pullover of Icelandic wool; the erratic pattern of greys should merge into the lichen covered rocks. I will do most of my filming on my knees, or lying down, so forming as inhuman a shape as possible.

I have to find the female who was courting here in the spring but I am not concerned that she has not showed after three hours. I need time to immerse myself in her world, to become aware of the details, at one with the environment around me, in tune with the tides. I have to reassure the gulls and oystercatchers that moan and pipe at my threatening form. I search every nook and cranny, just as otters do, trying to develop an intimate knowledge of the shore. I try to think like an otter, develop an instinct for their presence, withdraw from human life. My mind must adapt to new impulses, develop sensitivity to new stimulae. My senses become alive, the powers of observation acute; the primitive hunter stirs within me.

I search for brown fur in brown seaweed and tell-tale ripples in the grey waves. I see an otter, distant still, but close the gap with speed and stealth. One mistake and I might be finished for the day; the worry is not knowing you have made the mistake. The otter is fishing below Kirkabister, about thirty yards offshore. It would be easy to sneak up during her twenty-five-second dives, but the wind is from the north west and I risk my scent reaching her. I circle round inland as I have done so often before, and creep down the sheep track to the headland.

I assume the otter I am stalking is the same as that seen along here in March, but it may not be. Otters have 'home ranges' of two to three miles on these shores, and the ranges overlap, not being exclusive to any one otter. Males travel more widely, maybe six miles or so, covering the ranges of two or three females, all of whom they will try to mate with when their time is come. On the only shore where such measurements have been carried out on Fetlar, there was about one otter for every three-quarters of a mile of coast, so there may be as many as five or more otters around my chosen shores. I will have to get to know them all, just so my attention can be focused on the one individual that I have chosen to try to habituate to my presence. She looked like a youngish animal, and could breed for the first time at two to three years old. If she mated successfully with the male in March, she might produce her first cubs in early June, her gestation period being about nine weeks. This would be a regular time for cubs in Shetland, but even here they are notoriously erratic, and elsewhere appear to be strictly non-seasonal breeders.

Grey clouds follow one another across the voe, finally meeting overhead to become as one; light drizzle starts. Just when I begin to feel a move is overdue an otter peers over the rocks only thirty feet to my left. I have not been discovered yet, but it is certainly checking up and down the coast for danger. It appears to be my female, young looking and pale faced. The top lip marks and indistinct chest marking confirm my suspicions; I have found the courting female again. She relaxes after turning back and forth, lies down and starts to groom, partially hidden by a ridge of barnacle-covered rock. She seems uneasy, fidgeting constantly and frequently looking around for danger. Perhaps she is catching my scent a little, but just as I am considering risking a move, she walks down the rock and slips into the sea, paddling offshore to fish.

She seems to be a lethal hunter. After only three dives she catches what looks like a butterfish or an eel pout – forty yards out I cannot be sure – and for the next half an hour she catches similar species virtually every dive, fifteen in all, and eats the lot. I have to follow as I watch, for between each dive, she swims a few yards along the coast towards Dals Burn. She hunts the kelp beds which lie between twenty and fifty yards offshore, the water being perhaps thirty feet deep at the far edge of the kelp, shallower over most of it. She does not seem to venture out any further, for beyond that the voe drops away into the deeps, having been gouged out by an Ice Age glacier. Where she fishes was once dry land, for this is a recently drowned coastline, flooded by melting ice.

She swims towards shore, head half submerged. As she raises her head for a breath I realise she is carrying a fish in her mouth. She heads towards a small rocky promontory to the east – I am still some way off, but rushing closer is difficult, for her breathing times are erratic when carrying a fish, and the periods when she submerges are brief. When she is within ten yards of the shore she sinks gently out of sight, reappearing a moment later in the weed by the promontory. She is hiding, only her nose and eyes above the surface as she checks nervously around the shore. I go undetected, and she climbs on to the rocks with her prize, a ten inch sea scorpion, a large-headed, small-bodied yellow fish with attractive red markings, particularly on the disproportionately large pectoral fins. She appears to enjoy eating this fish, for she holds it between her webbed paws and chews with such concentration that she closes her eyes. I take my chance to move closer, crouching as low as I can in the weed covered rocks and settle silently just fifteen yards away. She alternates between right and left molars, crushing and sucking the fish in powerful jaws until the meal is almost complete. The tail section is last to go, devoured whole by throwing back her head and swallowing.

Feeding complete, she looks around before climbing up the shore to spraint, stepping from rock to rock with fluid grace. She selects a prominent stone near the high water mark, and spraints, tail stretched out. She is returning to the sea when suddenly she is aware of me. Neck stretched, eyes popping and nostrils flared, she bobs and weaves her head, 'snuffing' audibly, taking deep anxious breaths in order that she may better smell my scent. Satisfied that the shape and smell represents danger, she shoots down the rocks and plunges into the sea like a torpedo, leaving only a trail of bubbles behind her. She surfaces some forty yards along the shore, treading water and stretching her neck to improve her vision, seemingly unable to believe what she saw and requiring confirmation. Satisfied, she dives again and disappears.

After two more hours of waiting and searching without success, the tide is full, rain and wind increase; I head home to Mid Yell.

* * *

Dawn is slow to appear, the sky hardly lightening for hours; Shetland is blanketed in fog. Sea and sky, field and croft – all are transformed to a uniform dark grey. Visibility is virtually nil, but I am keen to keep tabs on my female and ensure that my presence on the shore is as permanent as the rocks in which I hide. I am unlikely to see anything of the otters, but alert to the fact that I may well hear something. She may even smell me, and then I will be a day nearer her accepting my scent.

The grass is dripping with the air's moisture, and every otter's footstep shows up on the stream edge. A cross country traveller has been down Dals Burn towards the sea, the route just discernible from the way the blades of grass are bent over. I wonder which otter was active in the night.

Upon reaching the shore I head east towards Kirkabister, using ears rather than eyes in the fog. At first all I hear is the mournful cry of a golden plover on the moorland to my left. The sea is still, wind and tide appear motionless, all activity cancelled for the day. I know this cannot be, and as my ears become tuned to fewer decibels than the human world, I become aware of water splashes, suspended somewhere between here and infinity. The noises sound close in the silence. One is certainly a jumping sea trout, another something larger, a shag or seal; an otter perhaps? I time the splashes and the gaps between dives suggest a fishing otter. Twenty to thirty seconds between noisy dive and quiet surfacing with about ten seconds rest between dives; I am sure it is an otter.

. . . she selects a prominent stone near the high water mark, and spraints . . .

I am able to keep abreast of it by listening to the sound: whichever direction in which it appears to fade, I follow. When the splashes stop I become tense. Has the otter given me the slip, or is it coming ashore in

front of me? There is silence. I sense the otter has moved and don't know which way, but as they tend to move in one direction during their feeding sprees of half an hour or so, I carry on towards Kirkabister.

I move in a lost world, returning to a time when man and animal were as one together. There is a magic in being here when no living creature is aware of my presence; in the dense fog the usual ripple of reaction and fear does not travel before me.

I walk slowly for twenty minutes, being careful not to break the silence with my footfalls. Just before I reach Kirkabister I become aware of a crunching noise in the kelp, just behind me. I turn quickly, and there is my otter again, eating a fish just twenty yards away; I have walked right past her. I am pleased my mode of travel is now so smooth and silent that I can walk close to an otter, but annoyed my eyes let me down – I was lucky she was preoccupied. She completes her lump sucker meal without alarm, then walks back over the weed to the sea. She must be smelling my scent in the still air, so close am I, but she does not even look back as she slips smoothly through the floating wrack, hesitates for a moment as if deciding where to fish next, and swims off out into the voe.

I follow the noise of her dives as she heads back towards Dals Burn, but they grow fainter and I finally lose her round the red garnet headland. Wind and tide rise but still the fog does not lift. I creep away from the shore.

. . . she takes the long deep breaths of sleep . . .

Next day I go through the standard routine yet again, down the hill, along the burn, check the sprainting spots and mud on the mini estuary, creep round the point, check the shore toward Sellafirth. There are fresh spraints, but only old prints in the mud. I scan the shore to the east and there is an otter, fishing offshore just beyond the old fence. I close in as quickly as the dives allow, and the otter lands just to the east of the large rocks, dragging ashore a large octopus. It seems to enjoy this meal, standing on it to subdue some of the clinging tentacles, and eating each in turn. I move closer and confirm that this is my female. Having finished eating the tentacles, she starts on the body and I wonder how she will deal with the ink sack. She is either not aware or not concerned at the hazard, for within moments she reels back, shaking her head and trying to wipe the ink off with her front paws. She alternates her rubbing from side to side, all the while shaking her head and 'snuffing' in obvious distress at the smell. After a few moments of this amusing behaviour she eats the rest of the octopus until there is not even a smear on the bladder wrack; I wonder if she is feeding more than one, and has cubs hidden in a holt somewhere. Meal completed, she has an enthusiastic groom, but still shakes her head in displeasure at the octopus ink. She then opens her mouth wide, and using one of her front claws, removes some of the remnants of the meal from between her teeth.

Apparently not satisfied by what I assumed was a large enough meal for an otter, she fishes on her way up the coast towards Kirkabister, catching a hat-trick of butterfish just offshore. I lose her round the point, and in a hurry to make a phone call, break all the rules and walk back along the cliff top. I am well pleased, for I discover the reason why the otter has so frequently given me the slip in the area of the garnet headland. There is a holt at the top of the low cliff, not discernible from the beach, but easily reached by a rock-climbing otter, and as it is midway between Dals Burn and Kirkabister, I call it the 'Halfway Holt'.

* * *

The next day is grey, the far side of the voe lost in mist, sea and shore stilled in a rare absence of wind. I wait by Halfway Holt for the tide to stir.

I am suddenly alert, aware of a movement round the point, a ripple on the calm. A pair of red-breasted mergansers appear, swimming towards me as they fish, oblivious of my crouching form. They search for small fry by swimming with just their eyes submerged, pushing a miniature bow wave with their foreheads. They see me when only a few yards away but as I am motionless, all they do is raise necks and crests, move a couple of yards further offshore, and then continue their search up the coast.

I wait an hour before I notice a fulmar is behaving oddly in its tours up and down the shore. Just this side of Kirkabister it falters in its flight, looking down into the rocks as it turns. The first time it does so my consciousness is hardly aroused, but a second time in the same spot spells sleeping otter; the apparently lifeless coast is not.

There is no wind as such, but the air drifts from the west, bearing my scent. I traverse half a mile to the east before starting to climb down the cliff but by the time I have finished my crawl the breeze has shifted to the east, and the object of the fulmar's attention is now looking at me, flanks taut and nostrils flared. She is concerned, but not unduly alarmed and slips into the sea without a backward glance.

She surfaces not far offshore and looks at me with wide eyes, then literally sinks out of sight, a little ring of bubbles being the only evidence of her presence. I would normally have expected to lose her now, but I notice her some way offshore, lying motionless on the surface, virtually indistinguishable from the miniature wavelets that disturb the calm. She is all but submerged, but I can just make out the shape of her head, part of her tail, and her left hip, for she has twisted her body so her legs are spread to one side. I get the impression she is sleeping. Motionless, she drifts slowly away in the tide and is lost in the wavelets. I strain my eyes, fondly imagining I can still see her, but she has given me the slip again.

Not wanting to drive her away from this coast altogether, I make an obvious departure up the coast past Kirkabister, hoping she is watching, intending to trick her into thinking I have gone.

Waiting hidden by the farm for even half an hour is difficult; I am impatient to return and try to find her again. Resolve weakening, I creep down the sheep track and start along the shore towards the spot I last saw her, tense but hopeful, stopping every few yards to search with binoculars each niche in rock and weed. I have almost reached the garnet headland when I notice her to my left. No need for binoculars now, she is just twenty yards away, sleeping on a small reef a few feet from the edge of the tide, curled up in a tight ball, snug on an ochre ledge. I drop to my knees, and shuffle as quietly as possible down the beach, but she makes it difficult, opening her eyes frequently and looking around as she adjusts her position. I imagine she cannot be comfortable where she lies, for the rocks are lined with barnacles, but when she does close her eyes, she takes the long deep breaths of sleep.

OVERLEAF LEFT
. . . she starts to groom . . .

RIGHT
. . . on her nose is a slight scar, raw pink . . .

It takes me half an hour to move body and camera to within fifteen feet of her slumbering form. She gives me an occasional myopic gaze, for her head is facing me. I am careful not to move when her eyes are open, but even if her eyesight is poor, her sensitive nose must surely smell me. She takes no notice of my close proximity; perhaps the 'peregrine technique' is really working.

We have both been motionless for what seems an age when she grows increasingly restless. Thankfully it is the splashing from the rising tide that disturbs her, not me. She starts to groom, scratching herself on back and stomach, then raising her nose to the sky, scratches energetically under her chin, eyes closed in apparent pleasure. Her long, sensitive whiskers, so vital when she hunts among the weedy rocks, vibrate during this enthusiastic grooming. The lip spots and the pale smudge on her chest show up clearly. She licks her tail from narrow tip to broad base, the shape of it flattened for maximum thrust when hunting. Both front and back legs are short but muscular, her hind quarters being particularly powerful. Tail cleaning complete she stands, hump backed, looks up and down the coast, gives me a glance, then slips into the water. I assume this to be the end of the close encounter, for whenever she has entered the water before, her poor eyesight has been transformed to something rather sharper. I wonder if the film of water improves the eyes' optical qualities; if such a thing is possible.

Instead of melting away, she swims across the narrow stretch of water between reef and shore and climbs out close to where I crouch. She sees me now and freezes, one paw held above the ground in arrested motion. I am amazed and delighted when she does not flee, but stands staring at me, fur sleek with seawater, dripping from chin and belly. She is so very tense even her whiskers seem to quiver and no muscle moves within me either – I hardly dare breathe. Perhaps this is the critical test, the watershed, where I am no longer rejected as foe, but accepted as part of the shore. She cocks her head to see me better, sniffs me nervously a few times, then walks slowly up the beach, selecting a flattish rock on which to spraint.

Scent marking complete she walks down the beach, glancing casually to east and west, looking through me as if I am finally accepted. I have been utterly still for some time. Perhaps I have grown invisible at last, witnessing nature in its natural form, avoiding the inevitable influence of my presence on her behaviour.

She slips into the sea, then back on to the offshore reef, shaking vigorously as she regains the comfort of her barnacle encrusted ledge. The texture of the fur on head and shoulders is spiky now, stuck together in bunches by the remaining moisture. She circles twice, in the manner of a dog, before lying on her back for another groom. She wriggles into a weed-covered crack, and scratches her back to and fro, legs flailing the air. Perhaps the remnants of moulting hair still bother her, for July is the time of her major change of coat. She will have another partial moult in November, a final preparation for winter; the thick waterproof pelt is adequate protection against even the coldest winter.

She has two layers of fur, one a dense inner coat, the outer consisting of longer guard hairs. She lies against a rock and grooms her stomach, the soft, silky lustrous hair teased out by her teeth. She is almost entirely covered by this pale brown fur, for her nugget brown skin only shows on the soles of her webbed paws and her small, rounded nose. Her coat can look reddish brown at times, contrasting strikingly with the pale fawn of her face and neck.

Of her assets for survival, smell is the strongest protection, but her small ears are also extremely sensitive and her long whiskers, sprouting profusely from both upper and lower jaw, provide aid when hunting along the weedy shore, or searching under boulders. On the right hand side of her nose is a slight scar, raw pink, a nip from a crab maybe, the biter bit!

I am tempted to give her a name, but I would then risk inflicting human values on a wild animal. Perhaps I do that anyway, just by filming or writing about her, but I am reluctant to be guilty of a breach of trust with such a beautiful creature and she just remains 'my otter'. She continues to groom vigorously for several minutes and I search her anatomy for clues of cubs. She does not appear unduly fat, and her four teats do not look particularly distended. Perhaps I shall have to wait another year before she produces, or maybe pregnancy does not show on otters, for certainly the

OVERLEAF ABOVE LEFT
. . . watching me drowsily at first . . .

RIGHT
. . . then she stretches her head out on the wrack and falls asleep . . .

BELOW
. . . his head fringed by a delicate feathery wig of weed . . .

little cubs, usually only two in number, are less than a foot long when born, and weigh only a few ounces.

I am suddenly aware that her vigorous activity has stopped, and she stares down the coast towards Dals Burn. I look too, and notice an otter, swimming unhurriedly towards us. It is the male, his broad muzzle and flared nostrils reflected in the still water as he travels along, pushing a little bow wave in front of his blunt features. His eyes are closed as he swims, totally relaxed until he is alongside me and catches my scent. He freezes, staring at me, eyes and nostrils flared, his back hidden by a patch of kelp, head fringed by a delicate feathery wig of weed. A few seconds is enough to convince him I represent danger, and then he just sinks out of sight, leaving barely a ripple. He is close to the reef on which the female grooms and though I hear no vocalisation he manages to transmit his fear to her. Without even a backward glance she slithers smoothly over the rock and into the sea, leaving only bubbles at the edge of the tide. The place suddenly feels very empty without her and I curse the male's meddling in our mutual trust.

After ten minutes of inactivity I notice an otter swimming along the sea edge, already more than a hundred yards away. Whilst watching it disappear round the headland below Kirkabister I notice a movement in the wrack at the reef edge. The female has returned to her grooming spot, and after a moment's foraging in the shallows, climbs back out on to her ledge, barely bothering to give me a glance. Relieved the male's alarm has not damaged her confidence, I stay with her as she rests fitfully. She becomes increasingly wet in the rising tide, and eventually slips into the water and heads down the coast towards Dals Burn. I follow closely, but lose her near the burn mouth. The bay is wide here and she may have cut across to the headland beyond. I search there but find no sign. If she does have cubs she has left me no clues today.

✳ ✳ ✳

Next morning I find the male out on the headland by Dals Burn. He alternates between fishing, grooming and sleeping. I keep well away, fearful of his nervous state, and avoid frightening him. After some two hours he heads east across the bay, and as I follow I see my female heading towards him. They both dive, then surface facing each other, have a brief roll with noses touching, then head their separate ways. I wonder at the significance of this brief meeting, and the affection they show for each other.

Over the next four days I see less and less of my female but the greeting between her and the male is repeated in much the same place on two more days. I search widely for signs that the female has cubs, but she proves elusive and I suspect she may have given birth and be nursing cubs in some unknown holt. It is usually eleven to twelve weeks after birth before cubs are brought out for the first time so I may still have several weeks to wait. I have only one more day before heading south to Dorset and reluctantly accept that I shall not see cubs during this visit. I must satisfy myself with the knowledge that I seem to have broken through the barrier of fear that lay between me and one very special otter.

✳ ✳ ✳

I am on the shore early, keen to make the best of this last bright, sunny day. There is little wind, and I walk back and forth along the shore, enjoying the unexpected warmth of a Shetland summer. I suppose I do not really anticipate seeing my female again, so elusive has she been, and I walk for several hours, happy to remember the brief moments of trust she has allowed me. I try the headland below Dals Burn one last time and rounding the point I see her fishing offshore. She busies herself with butterfish as I work myself down to the edge of the sea, crouching in the water in order to be close to her.

When she finally notices me between dives, she swims towards me, inquisitive now at the persistent form that pursues her day after day. She is hesitant at first, watching me from a few feet away, but having checked my

scent, swims right up. I cannot believe this is happening, a wild otter on a wild Shetland shore, looking at me, fearless, just three feet away. I reach out to try to stroke her on the head, but she will not allow me this final liberty in our relationship, and sinks out of sight.

She surfaces just to my left, and climbs ashore, looking at me with natural curiosity, snuffing with jerking head. She is $3\frac{1}{2}$ feet long, but looks diminutive in this large, wild landscape and its wide horizons. She re-enters the water, circles round me, then climbs out the other side, walking closer, as if to be sure of recognising me again. Still wet from the sea, her coat glistens as she watches me in the midday sun. In this wonderful moment of trust, I vow to remember this privilege forever.

She swims close to me once more, swerving with infinite grace around the tangle at my feet, before climbing out on the rocks just to the east. She settles down, watching me drowsily at first, but finally stretches her head out on the wrack and falls asleep. I withdraw silently up the beach, leaving her to rest. I creep towards Dals Burn and look back for a last glimpse of her, but shore and sea are empty; only my memories drift on the tide.

CHAPTER 5

Tragedy

SEPTEMBER 17TH. Dawn is cloudless, the sun sharp with brilliance. Walking east, I shield my eyes. Out in the bay seals create silver ripples on the dark surface; I am confident my otter will announce her presence in the calm. Perhaps on this visit she will show me if she really does have cubs.

I find I now hold a real affection for her, as one might for a pet cat or dog, but I accept reluctantly that this affection is not likely to be returned. She has certainly become more confiding over the months but each time I return I wonder if she will recognise me.

I walk past Kirkabister, out on to the headland, listening to the thin fluting whistle of the whimbrel, so clear and pure in the rising skies of morning. There is a wonderful wildness about the place, a sense of space and freedom which other more populated and pressurised countryside now lacks. This place has the essence of wilderness, constantly elevating.

I climb the hillside with the sun, revelling in this world of wind and sky. Finches bound south down the wind, leaving in their wake a sprinkling of song. Waiting for winter, hooded crows watch the whimbrel depart for the salty creeks of the African coast; their fluty whistles sound happy, as if in celebration of their leaving. Autumn is not a season of melancholy, for it carries with it hope for the wonders of winter.

There is a luminous light, no wisp of cloud, the distant Out Skerries standing out sharp against the eastern sky. It is clear, so clear, too clear maybe, for I have the uneasy feeling it is the forerunner of rain. I am anxious for success, and time may be running out. I retrace my steps and there in the sand is a solitary print; she has crossed my path and gone, leaving no trace on the stony ground to either side.

I long to see her again, but in not seeing I am not disappointed. Her very presence, the fact she watches me with her watery eyes, that is enough; I am content she is still here. It is as if some effort should be expended before I am ready for a reunion, that I am not yet deserving of such good fortune.

Passing round Hivdigan Headland I suddenly become aware of an indefinable 'presence' behind me. I swivel round, and there in a peaty hollow in the cliff stands a magnificent male peregrine, glaring at me defiantly, reluctant to leave his starling meal. In a moment he is gone, flying across the voe in a seemingly effortless few strokes of his streamlined muscular wings, taking his prey with him. Remembering him as the inspiration for my otter filming technique, I wonder if his appearance is symbolic, and if he carries a message in his talons.

It cannot be, for my otter remains undiscovered for three more days.

❊ ❊ ❊

A fresh northerly wind springs up overnight and lowering black clouds hang over the hill behind Dals Burn. I search the shore in some comfort, sheltered by the cliff from the wind and the worst of the rain squalls. They sweep across the voe from north to south, following the migrant birds. As if she has always been there, I discover my female asleep on the shore below the garnet headland. It is low water, and she lies curled up, head resting on tail, far down the beach. I risk my scent reaching her in the offshore wind and creep slowly down towards her. She looks up at me, unconcerned at first, but then she departs.

I do not wish to alarm her unduly, and in the hope she will lead me to her cubs I let her get some way ahead before attempting to follow. She swims west past the Halfway Holt, on down the shore past the large rocks she so likes to spraint at, then through the old fence. I am some distance behind now and grow anxious as she draws away. I scan the bay, thinking she has cut across to Dals Burn Headland but there is no sign of her. She has either given me the slip in the rough water, or cut inland up the burn. I search there for recent signs of her passage but the mud and grass banks seem undisturbed. I return to the shore and scan from behind the peat blocks, but the sea appears empty. Her regular disappearance here is a mystery, for I have looked inland on the moor and there are no holts there. Then I have it. Walking thoughtfully along I suddenly realise I have always been searching sea and shore hereabouts, with my back to the peat bank. Turning round, there before me is the perfect holt, a narrow vertical slit high up in the peat, the entrance smoothed and scratched by the frequent toing and froing of an otter. There are fresh spraints on a large tuft of grass outside, but just to make sure the holt is in regular use I smooth the entrance with a piece of driftwood. This way I will leave no trace of my scent, but my female will leave tell-tale marks in the peat. I withdraw, convinced she is sleeping inside, with cubs perhaps? I wait some distance away until dusk closes around me but nothing stirs at the holt's entrance. I christen it the Burn Bank Holt and, pleased with events, walk home to bed.

❊ ❊ ❊

I am in the area again before night's shadows clear the northern shore. I creep along Dals Burn in the half light, my senses prickly with anticipation. Hardly daring to move, expecting to see a head appear from the entrance at any moment, I reach the Burn Bank Holt and find fresh scratch marks on the smoothed-out peat; at least one otter has been in or out during the night, but nothing stirs this morning. After a long and fruitless wait I walk east towards Kirkabister, searching for my female.

I reach the farm without incident, and rest in my hiding place below the cliff. The tide has been ebbing for some time before I see the vee of a bow wave approaching from the west, swimming slowly towards me and diving at intervals. An almost mystical sense of recognition convinces me it is my female. She swims on the surface with head and back showing, using her hind feet to propel her body with effortless grace. She dives occasionally using her front paws to steer and her back legs and tail for propulsion. Her body is silvered with air bubbles caught in her pelt, and these float to the surface in a chain, betraying the direction of her dive. It is a thrill to watch the slow, leisurely, graceful movement of a questing otter,

OVERLEAF LEFT
. . . the Burn Bank Holt, smoothed by the frequent toing and froing of otters . . .

ABOVE RIGHT
. . . she drags the eel on to the rocks . . .

BELOW RIGHT
. . . she feeds long and hard . . .

and a delight to be close to her again, identity confirmed, her whiskery features so familiar to my affectionate gaze.

After fishing unsuccessfully offshore for some time, she appears to struggle as she reaches the surface, rolling around uneasily and disappearing occasionally as if in combat. I see a large black tail alongside her momentarily, and realise she has caught a large conger eel which is proving difficult to subdue. It writhes energetically by her side as she tries to head for the shore, but after a protracted struggle she drags the eel on to the rocks and proceeds to eat the head of her dead prey. She feeds long and hard, chewing and sucking the eel with her large molars. She sits motionless, with eyes closed, and as I creep closer I realise she is asleep. She wakes only occasionally, sucking on her meal in the manner of a baby's dummy, but with her eyes still closed.

She wakes eventually, and is startled at my close proximity, retreating a

few feet across the weed, dragging her meal with her. I lie still at a point where she cannot see me, letting her calm herself before attempting to go closer, sharing these same rocks in silence. I feel close to her, seeing and smelling the salty tang of the seaweed on which she herself has slept.

I rise slowly, and aware now of where I am, she relaxes, as if the suspense of not knowing where I was had been what bothered her. I fondly imagine that she may now be considering me not as foe, but friend. In truth I know that such human values are not within the grasp of a wild otter, but I am moved by the trust this endearing creature shares with me.

She continues her meal, sleeping occasionally between more intensive bouts of eating. After a while she drops the fish, walks a few paces up the shore, spraints, then picks up her eel and heads hurriedly up the coast past Kirkabister. I wonder at the significance of this fish carrying, and rush after her, having difficulty keeping up as she swims east at an impressive pace. When she reaches the middle of the bay she cuts in towards the shore, and I hide against the bank for fear I might spoil my chances of discovering her cubs.

After checking briefly up and down the shore for danger, she drags the eel up the beach, climbs the bank where a small stream runs off the hill, and disappears. I rush forward, convinced now that I am just moments from my first view of her cubs.

The stream runs obliquely down the hill in a narrow valley, cut straight and deep in the peat. The water trickles through dense stands of soft rush and frequently becomes clogged in blankets of spagnum moss. I see her trail clearly through this green mass, but in places the stream plunges underground and its route is only discernible from the subterranean tinkling of water. I see the scratches from her journey but no sign of her cubs. I am in doubt as to whether to pursue her up the stream and risk frightening her, or hold back and hope to hear the cubs from down the hill. I wait as long as my curiosity allows, but hearing nothing, I head up the hill to try to find a holt.

Some two hundred yards above the beach the stream divides, and as the otter's trail appears more obvious to the north east, I follow this tributary. Fifty yards further on there is a shallow hollow in the hill and the stream appears briefly on the surface, disappearing on either side into dark peaty holes. They are lined attractively with delicate green ferns and mosses, and are worn smooth by the frequent passage of otters. The grass on the banks is flattened by their activity – perhaps they play and groom here, but I cannot find the place she might be hiding cubs, so try the main stream to the north west.

Ottery scratches in the peat and fresh spraints raise my hopes as I climb the hill, and then I find the holt in the peat bank at the edge of the steam. The earthworks are extensive, and two of the holes lead directly into the underground stream, perfect for undetected escape. I retreat downwind and lie on the hillside for an hour or two but see no movement, and hear no sounds. Suspecting she has detected me tracking her, I return to the shore and make myself comfortable under the cliff with some old fish boxes and driftwood. Above me is a ruined cottage with its own little stream, once the site of a small mill; one of the stones lies on its side in the sand. The house was called Longadykes, no doubt named after the streams I have just searched. I christen the holt I have discovered, not very originally, Hill Holt, and sit on my fish box until dark. Nothing stirs.

✳ ✳ ✳

Two more dawn and dusk vigils reveal nothing and my female remains hidden. I have to return south on another assignment, so Bobby takes over my fish box hide for several evenings. He too sees nothing, and the whereabouts of my otter's cubs, if she has any, remain a mystery.

✳ ✳ ✳

The ferry crossing from Aberdeen on October 23rd is rough. I hang on to the edge of the bed, bracing myself as the boat tosses and bucks in the swell; books, papers and briefcase slide back and forth across the cabin floor.

Upon arrival I catch up with Bobby and Betty's news. The only otter cubs that have been reported were sighted at the head of Mid Yell Voe, so I set off immediately on a protracted search. The reports sounded slightly ambiguous and the lack of fresh spraints or suitable holts or lie-ups convinces me I should return to Basta Voe to see what my female is up to.

I walk hurriedly down Dals Burn – the light is falling fast but I am confident amongst so much familiarity. There are fresh spraints on the banks; I creep low along the shingle, jump the burn, and peer round the headland to the west. I immediately notice a gull standing on the shore, then just beyond it, after a long search in the half light, the furry form of a sleeping otter; when I reach the spot the otter is gone; the gull flies off, calling in alarm.

I return quickly to the headland and find the otter grooming at the edge of the sea. I recognise her, although she looks very fat when she stands to re-enter the water, her teats appear distended. I watch with anticipation as she fishes just offshore, and my optimism leaps as she catches a small butterfish on her fourth dive and instead of eating it, swims past close to me, the fish wriggling in her jaws. She moves purposefully, her direction obvious, as if she is anxious I should share her secret. I follow to the east, past Dals Burn, and she climbs ashore just below the Burn Bank Holt, still carrying the fish. She hesitates briefly, looking carefully up and down the coast for danger, but ignores me, walks swiftly up the beach and climbs into the holt. After many weeks of effort I have finally fulfilled my ambition to see an otter enter a holt; maybe I am within minutes of fulfilling my other ambition and will see her cubs.

. . . only a soft glow of light is left in the western sky . . .

I risk moving closer so that I can use the peat blocks for cover, and have not been hidden long before she appears through a hole in the roof of the

holt. From this high vantage point on top of the bank, she checks all around for danger, jerking her head as she sniffs for hostile scent. She then ducks back into the holt, her head reappearing out of a small hole high up on the bank, closer to me than the main entrance. She looks very alert, but drops down on to the beach, turning immediately to look back up at the hole. To my relief and utter delight, a little whiskery face appears, squeaking loudly, hesitant about dropping down to the beach below. With encouragement from mother it slithers down the bank, on to Mum's back and then on to the beach. It is a most delightful fluffy chestnut brown ball, short in neck and leg, rotund in body and head, a perfect miniature otter. The sense of elation is immense and I shout silently in glorious celebration of success. After all these weeks of walking I have finally found my otter cubs.

No sooner has the first cub reached the beach than a second appears at the hole, even more hesitant than the first. It finally falls out of the hole, trying to drop down on to its mother's back, but misses, and lands in a heap at the bottom of the bank, chittering with surprise and alarm. When it gets to its feet Mum leads both cubs down the beach, stopping to spraint on the way; she encourages the cubs to do the same by nudging their behinds.

The moon rises above the voe, a thin sliver, visible through lingering wisps of cirrus. It is nearly dark now. Only a chink of light is left in the western sky, but this is reflected in the calm water at the edge of the beach. I see my female break this mirror of the night sky, but the cubs stand on the shore, hesitant silhouettes, squeaking as their mother fishes offshore. She works her way east into night's shadow, followed by the cubs. I withdraw into the darkness too, full of optimism for tomorrow.

As I drive towards Dals Burn, snow buntings flicker white in the car headlights, suggesting winter is on the way, but I am in no doubt it has already arrived when I open the car door, and am greeted by a stinging sleet shower, driven on by strong north easterly winds. Once I reach the cover of the cliff, the dawn is not uncomfortable, for the high ground behind me shelters the first few yards of the sea, creating a narrow strip of calm water; it stretches up the coast towards the first of the day's light, shimmering silver in the squalls. It is already 7.15, but the rest of the voe hides in the darkness of lingering night.

I wait near the Burn Bank Holt for the skies to brighten, then as no mother and cubs appear, walk east towards Kirkabister, hoping I might find them there. Just before I reach the garnet headland I notice my female sleeping at the edge of the sea. A shaft of sunlight breaches the dense clouds to the east and drifts down the shore; as it reaches my otter's curled-up form she glows golden brown on her bed of lush green seaweed. She catches my scent and looks at me sleepily. Disturbed, she grooms energetically, interspersing her ablutions with several wide-mouthed, toothy yawns. Awake now, she slips effortlessly into the rising tide, and swims slowly east towards Kirkabister. The sun is bright now, the sea a palest yellow. Each wavelet is bright blue but offshore where the surface is more broken by the wind, the sea only reflects the blue of the sky. Relaxing too much in all this wild beauty, I lose the female somewhere amongst the reefs below Kirkabister. I suspect she has headed round the bay towards Burraness; perhaps she has climbed up the stream to the Hill Holt? I go to check but there are no signs fresh enough to erase the conviction that I should be somewhere in the area of Dals Burn; I cannot imagine the female travelling this far with such small cubs. I retrace my steps to the Burn Bank Holt, find a comfortable tuft of grass below the cliff, and sit down, prepared for a long wait.

As the hours pass the squalls become less frequent, the skies clear, the wind drops. By lunchtime it is a really fine day, and I am happy where I sit. Some hunch convinces me that I am waiting for the cubs in the right place and long, bitter experience tells me that the difference between success and failure lies with my instinct being correct. Success depends simply on being in the right place at the right time, but with otters it is difficult to know whether you are in the right place at the wrong time, or in the wrong place at the right time! By 2.30 in the afternoon, after I have waited six hours, the first nagging pangs of self-doubt are beginning to gnaw at my confidence. The last time I saw the female she was more than half a mile away, and I have seen nothing of her since.

I relieve the growing tension by watching a family of wrens gathering spiders under the peat overhang of the cliff. Most of them still show yellow gapes, diagnosing them as recently fledged young, and I discover their vacated nest in a crevice in the peat. The adults suddenly call in alarm and the atmosphere is electrified. Why did they call? I fix my concentration on the entrance to the holt and moments later a rush of water runs out of the rain-soaked hole, followed almost immediately by the face of my female. She pokes only her head out, checking to left and right for danger. I think I am undetected, but she retreats back into the holt and ten tense minutes of inactivity follow.

Next time she appears, she climbs right out of the holt and on to the sprainting ledge half way down the bank. She checks nervously to left and right, the wrens swearing loud abuse at her. She returns to the holt, reappears again briefly, then disappears inside. Moments later she appears out of the hole in the roof of the holt, followed closely by the cubs. She walks quickly along the top of the bank to a shallow gully, the cubs running bouncily at her heel. She climbs down easily, but the cubs once again have to jump on to her back to break their fall. One cub is noticeably smaller, and is hesitant before it jumps, remembering perhaps the accident last night. It whimpers slightly, but descends successfully, and all three spraint on a broken block of peat. The cubs just wee, and being close by I notice that the larger does so forwards, the smaller backwards; they are brother and sister.

Their mother leads them down the beach, looking back to make sure they are with her. She enters the water immediately, but the two little cubs stand at the water's edge, squeaking their penetrating whistle at the female. They can only be two and a half months old, so small and fluffy are they, and this would be one of their first expeditions out of the holt. Perhaps they have yet to experience the water, for they are hesitant and anxious. Their mother returns to encourage them, climbs out of the sea, and walks close to the cubs. Her son follows her into the sea, but little sister stands on the edge squeaking, then turns and runs back up the beach towards the holt. Her mother and brother run up the beach after her, fuss around her for a moment, then all three walk across the shingle and into the sea.

They swim in the shallowest water at the edge, one cub on either side of their mother. They are extremely buoyant, their fluffy coats acting as a form of lifejacket. They paddle along, heads clear of the water, but are unable to follow their mother when she dives for fish, so circle round nose to tail, squeaking intermittently. They drift slowly west past Dals Burn, their mother frequently returning to reassure them and to look around for danger. She moves slowly offshore, and they follow for several yards. When she dives the male cub ducks his head under the water, no doubt watching his mother hunting in the weed below, but when his sister tries this, she gets water up her nose and quickly splutters to the surface, shaking her head and paddling for the shore. Her mother heads towards her with a little butterfish, which she grabs greedily, and despite the competition from her brother, chews and swallows the complete fish herself. She has been too greedy and like a small human child, promptly sicks the fish up. Her brother rushes forward for the half chewed fish, but she has already re-swallowed it. Weaning on to solids will have started a few weeks ago, but the cubs will still be suckled by their mother until they are about fourteen weeks old.

OVERLEAF ABOVE LEFT
. . . she attempts to use her son as a pillow . . .

BELOW LEFT
. . . the cubs climb over her and try to suckle . . .

RIGHT
. . . she tries to hide by lying on top of him . . .

The cubs are fed three more fish on the headland beyond Dals Burn, then the family walk up the beach and investigate the holes in the broken peat bank, climbing in and out inquisitively. They spraint on the bank top before cutting down the headland to the west, and swim through the weed towards the pier-like promontory of rock on which the male so often rests. I rush forward with the camera in anticipation, for I have heard that males are not tolerated anywhere near a mother with cubs, even if he is their father.

The family climb out on to the promontory and the female immediately walks purposefully forward round the large rock. There is a sudden explosion of fur as the male is surprised in his resting place. She lunges at him with open mouth, whickering angrily, and he stands up on his back legs to defend himself. With amazing speed they lash each other with their teeth, trying to fend off the attacks with their front paws. Squealing loudly, he retreats quickly into the sea, no match for a nursing mother. As he flees, he knocks one of the cubs off the rock into the sea, but it seems unhurt as it climbs back up to its mother. She ignores both cubs for a moment, sniffing busily around the rock where the male slept, and sprainting on the spot as if to make her point. The male quickly heads west round the sandy Ayre of Cunnister, out of sight.

Honour satisfied, the female slowly relaxes and lies down with the cubs at the seaward end of the promontory. They climb over her and try to suckle, and she attempts to use her son as a pillow. He wriggles out from under her head, jumps on his sister playfully, then they both wrestle about on top of her, trying to bite each other's faces. Thus for five minutes they fidget about and successfully disrupt Mum's attempt at slumber. She suddenly stands up, tumbling the cubs into the seaweed, walks across the rocks and checks once again the scene of the fight, perhaps to make sure the male has not returned. She returns to the cubs and lies down again, her coat glowing yellowish in the crisp sunshine. Behind her the sea is dark grey, warning of an approaching squall.

Mercifully the storm passes to the west, and the family enter the sea to fish again. Mum works her way towards me and the cubs follow on the shore. She suddenly becomes alarmed at my presence and lies motionless in the weed, watching me from under a floating frond of bladder wrack. Her attempt at hiding is completely destroyed, for the cubs swim over and climb on to her head!

She swims offshore and starts to fish, trusting me with the cubs, who circle around in the rough water, coats spiky with moisture. They each have two little hairs sticking out from the tops of their foreheads, like radio antennae, and these glisten with drops of moisture. She returns to the rocky promontory, giving me a cursory glance as she climbs out of the water, hurriedly, for the cubs rush to grab the butterfish she carries in her mouth. Snatching this way and that, and standing on one leg with neck stretched high, she avoids their lunges, and eats the fish herself. She then lies on her back to groom, and thinking this a perfect invitation for a romp, the cubs rush across the weed and jump on to her. She gently bats then off one by one with her front paw.

They rest for some time, then she heads offshore to fish. The sea is calm now, reflecting the weary light of dying summer. The pattern of wind and wave is broken only by the bubbles and ripples of her dives, black on lemon yellow. The cubs wait on shore.

Across the voe, the southern shore falls into the shadow of the evening sky. It is bright to the east; black, heavy and threatening to the west. The sun pierces the cloud, casting holy rays of light across the sky. I creep down the beach and mother and cubs swim ashore with a small fish. She shakes herself vigorously, spraying water in sparkling droplets over the feeding cubs. She walks towards me, ignoring my presence; it is a wonderful feeling to be trusted. She spraints on a nearby rock, closing her eyes as she does so, then returns to the calm voe to fish.

The cubs suddenly realise she has gone and become alarmed when they realise how close I am. They hide under the weed on the shore, using various places, the little female even trying to hide behind her brother by lying on top of him. They relax quickly, and sit huddled together, eyes bright in the setting sun, watching their mother with longing.

Solar fire burns through the clouds, then sinks quickly behind the distant hills, the glowing red orb reduced to a thin red line, rippling faintly as it is overtaken by night. The moon follows it across the sky. Greylag geese pass overhead in the darkness, heralding the coming of winter. I leave the family curled up together, sleeping soundly.

✻ ✻ ✻

The wind has risen again by morning, blowing strongly from the north east. Sunny periods and showers turn the sea's surface yellow and grey, the

. . . the cubs become alarmed
when they realise how close I
am . . .

dominant colour depending on the position of the scudding clouds.

I find the family a few yards to the east of the Burn Bank Holt; fresh spraints suggest they have just come out. I follow them towards Kirkabister but my female is nervous this morning, my scent blowing down to her in gusts. I circle round to Kirkabister, and approaching from the other direction, move close to the family as they rest on a reef below the farm. They huddle on the rocks in a rainstorm, but are restless and continually climb back and forth into the sea, often leaving the little female cub behind, who is still hesitant about entering the water.

They swim very close, and Mum spots me and dives. The cubs try to follow her below, but despite much thrashing of front and back legs only succeed in submerging their heads and shoulders. Mum swims alongside them and they try to hitch a ride on her back. She swivels round, grabs one by the scruff of the neck, and dives a few feet back towards the reef; their first diving lesson perhaps, or just a response to my close proximity?

They return to the reef, the female lying on one cub, whilst the other climbs on top of her – an otter cub sandwich. The tide is flooding fast and soon washes them off the reef; they head west towards Dals Burn in a steel blue sea, the cubs moving at a surprising speed for ones so small. I follow quickly, but the rocks are wet from the rain and are as slippery as bars of soap. I lose my footing and fall heavily, managing to twist round as I drop so the camera lands on my neck instead of the rocks. The accident brings home to me how vulnerable I would be on this remote coast if a fall was more serious, but there is strange comfort in the fact that no living human knows exactly where I am . . . only my female otter.

Recovering from the fall, I re-find her to the east of Dals Burn, walking down the beach from some old rabbit burrows; I wonder how they squeezed into them. She settles the cubs amongst the large boulders, then brings them a small butterfish. The little female is quickest to the grab and gets the meal. Her mother then busies herself underneath the large rock, digging energetically with her front paws and kicking the shingle out with powerful back feet. Her son sits behind her and gets showered with missiles, ducking this way and that before finally retreating; I laugh at the comedy routine.

Having dug a small pit, she scours the beach, breaking off the bushiest bunches of bladder wrack with her teeth, and carrying them to the hollow under the rock. Satisfied, she encourages the cubs to settle in this nest, then heads out into the voe for a peaceful spell of hunting.

Evening closes in now, the sun shining weakly through the grey pall of cloud. It is low water, the sea silvery amongst the yellow fronds of kelp. The wind is blustery, but pools in the weed are sheltered, reflecting the pastel greys and whites of a watery sky. The cubs are too restless to remain in their nest for long, and paddle about in these pools, whistling for their mother. She obliges with several small fish and I retreat from the shore as the night sky starts to threaten rain.

✳ ✳ ✳

Wednesday October 29th is the wildest of days. A gale-force wind blows from the north west, heavy squalls of sleet sweep across Basta Voe and though there are sunny periods it feels really cold. I walk hard to keep warm, searching the windswept shore from Dals Burn to Kirkabister.

When I reach the farm there is an indefinable 'presence'. I creep forward, suspecting an otter is sleeping in the lie-up below the cliff. There are only fresh spraints there but the fish net is missing. Looking down into the rocks I notice the net under a rock, and curled up inside is the sleeping form of an otter. I try not to move but am already leaning on the cliff behind me, and dislodge a small stone. It clatters on to the rocks and the otter twists round, looking sleepily at me through a hole in the net. It is my female, but I am only a few feet from her and caught standing upright, out in the open, making a noise. She considers this a breach of trust and plunges into the sea, then rises half out of the water, neck stretched, staring wide-eyed at me, she decides she does not like what she sees, gives me a disapproving 'wuff' and disappears.

As it is nearly high water I decide to check round Burraness for other otters, but wind and squalls conspire to make viewing difficult and I see nothing.

Returning to Dals Burn, I hear the unmistakable squeaks of an otter cub in the patch of wild iris. I creep down to the burn edge, and wait where it enters the sea, expecting the family to appear from upstream. The cubs continue to squeak but their mother suddenly appears in the sea to my left. She takes a short cut up the shingle bank and I have to lie flat as she runs past me with a butterfish. Plunging into the stream, she disappears into the iris patch in a shower of bubbles.

The next thing I see is the family running over the hill to the west, humpbacked, mother leading, the cubs following behind like bouncy rubber toys. They are taking a short cut across the headland so I creep round along the shore, finding them already huddled together on an offshore rock. They clamber about on each other, and thus distracted I manoeuvre close to them, my movements covered by the noise of wind and wave. The male cub roots around on his mother's stomach and tries to suckle but she grabs him by the scruff of the neck and pulls him away. Thus frustrated he lies on his back, inviting his sister to play. She obliges, pouncing on him, and he kicks upwards with all four stubby legs in order to keep her off. They wrestle and bite for several minutes, squealing and whimpering in pain and delight. Wind and tide rise, and the cubs' activities are confined to an ever decreasing patch of rock.

The sunshine is harsh, the sea an unreal blue. White horses are whipped away from the shore by the squalls, and a sleet shower slashes hurriedly across the voe. The otter family, splashed continually by waves, give up their siesta and fish close inshore. The cubs bob buoyantly round and round, nose to tail, occasionally spluttering when swamped by a wave. They head east, following their mother, who, undetected by them, lands on a rock with a sea scorpion. She eats greedily, ripping and chewing the fish as if really hungry. The cubs drift away, but their calls rise above the noise of the waves and hearing them, she hurriedly completes her meal and heads along the shore to where she left them.

I grow anxious, for the cubs have been blown offshore and she is unaware of this, searching the water close to the rocks. Failing to find them, she rises up in the water and starts to call loudly. The cubs hear and try to swim to her but they can make no headway against the wind and mother and cubs are blown inexorably apart. I wish I had some way of telling her where they are. I even consider swimming out to them myself, but decide it is not worth drowning, even for the sake of two delightful otter cubs. Their calls grow ever fainter and their little bodies are now hardly visible in the spume.

My female dashes back and forth across Dals Burn Bay, flailing through the water, spray flying up from her shoulders as she powers through the waves. She calls loudly but the answering cries of her cubs blow away in the gale. I do not know if otters experience desperation and anguish but her demented search suggests they do.

I feel increasingly helpless and sad, reliving all those wonderful intimate moments I have shared with her. Now I am sharing the worst moment of her life, her first cubs drowned, and I can do nothing to help; I am near to tears. No longer able to watch, I try to creep away unseen so as not to disrupt her search, but she catches sight of me and comes rushing over. She is so used to my being close to her cubs that she looks around me for them, then stands and looks at me for a moment – understanding passes between us. I am touched by her trust and wish that in return I could help her, but failing to find the cubs, she plunges back into the sea and hurries up the coast towards Kirkabister. I lose sight of her in the waves.

I turn my back on the coast and am greeted by the most magnificent rainbow, curved vividly over the hill, incongruous in this moment of tragedy. But perhaps it carries a message of hope? Perhaps she will find her cubs and establish a new home range on some distant shore? She may even return here with them, but in my heart I know they are gone. The sky turns black. Another sleet shower drenches me and I climb wearily up the hill against the gale, despairing at the way fate has played against me, and against my wonderful little otter.

✳ ✳ ✳

I return to the shore at dawn, hoping desperately to find signs that the cubs survived, but there is an uncanny sense of lifelessness. Ironically, it is a lovely morning, the sea calm now, and frost glistens on marsh grass. It is as if the storm was a bad dream, the drowned cubs a nightmare, and in reality I shall find the family just round the next headland playing in the sun. But all I find is the male, eating a sea scorpion in the shallows.

Bobby searches the shores of Hascosay and Basta Voe from his boat but there is no sign of the family. I search the north shore until nightfall but there is no trace of either the cubs, or their mother. It seems the storm has

removed not only the little otter cubs but my special friend too. The feeling of emptiness and despair is complete and I leave Shetland depressed and defeated.

CHAPTER 6

Try, try again

IT IS May 25th before I return to Shetland to try to find my female otter again. A whole winter has passed, sufficient time, I hope, for her to return to the north shore of Basta Voe and mate with the resident male. If she has obliged, she may well have a new litter of cubs, but searching for her will have to wait, for a school of pilot whales has just appeared in the area, and I must try to take advantage of this good fortune.

The whales have moved north overnight from Basta Voe to the village of Uyeasound, a small settlement on the south coast of Unst. Fearful they will leave the islands completely, we hurriedly prepare our equipment after the long journey north, but it is lunchtime before Bobby's boat is loaded and we slip the moorings. The children are with us, for it is their half-term holidays; they are excited at the prospects and gaze out in anticipation over Hascosay Sound. The languid surfacing of porpoises creates a shout of false alarm, so they satisfy themselves by leaning over the bows, looking down through the crystal clear waters at the piltock-infested tangle below.

We head north east, slipping gently past the cliffs of Burraness, and I look longingly at the familiar bays and geos that have seen so much of my life go by. The boat begins to rock gently as we motor away from the ruined broch and out into the tide, scattering the feeding tysties in our path. Common seals watch us sleepily as we pass the rocky islet of Sound

Gruney; Unst looms on the horizon to the north. The day is calm but grey, the sky heavy with cloud; rain feels imminent. The horizon to the east is wide and bright, reflecting the ocean's finer climate. Tiny silhouettes of fishing boats stand out against the bright sky, and gannets dive close to them, piercing the lemon yellow sea.

We leave the uninhabited island of Uyea to the east, the ruin of the hall standing stark against the sky, a poignant reminder of more populated times. Vee Taing and the Wick of Brecknagarth slip past our stern as the land closes around us and the bay of Uyeasound opens up. Then we see the whales, distant at first, but their black backs unmistakable as they circle the bay in a tight school. They are an impressive sight, one hundred and fifty or so in number, unconcerned at our approach. The thrill of such a meeting is intense and the children rush about the deck in excitement.

The school circles peacefully in front of us, their black backs and dorsal fins creating only the slightest ripple, despite the bulk of over twenty feet of whale below the waves. The air is filled with the sound of their breathing, their blowholes raised briefly above the surface as they exhale hot air high into the sky. Clicks and squeaks punctuate their movements, which at first appear random but which certainly are not, for three large adult males place themselves between us and the rest of the school, and hold this station as we too circle around.

Nick Dymond, the RSPB warden on Fetlar, has come along to help, so while Bobby backs off with his boat, Nick rows me into the heart of the school in a ten foot dinghy. We feel no fear amongst such gentle creatures, only privilege. The school splits slightly, and we are surrounded, even from below. Some of the whales slide past so close we feel we could touch them, and others roll on their sides and look at us with their small but benevolent eyes. These moments of sheer delight are cut short by the appearance of a motor boat from Uyeasound, and we return to Bobby's boat to reduce the disturbance to the school.

The villagers circle the whales in awe just as we had done, but in times past their intentions would have been more sinister, for these whales are known locally as 'Caain Whales', meaning 'driven'. Even as recently as 1916, they were surrounded and driven ashore to be killed for their oil. Economic necessity and attitudes have changed, and the appearance of whales is now an excuse for celebration and sightseeing rather than butchery. As if in memory of less enlightened days, the whales become more animated at the appearance of the second boat and several raise their flukes high in the air and smash them on to the surface in a welter of spray, exploding water above the height of the nearby crofts. This display of energy and power is in marked contrast to their previous relaxed wallowing, and thinking the best is over we drift away down the tide, back home to Yell. Next morning the whales are gone.

* * *

A few spots of rain patter the surface of the voe, and a fresh south easterly riffles the grass at the cliff edge. High water is not until mid afternoon, so I delay the resumption of my search until 11 a.m. There are fresh otter tracks at the burn mouth and I wait on the headland. The sky is darker than the sea, but breaks appear in the cloud, creating a mood of optimism and changing the views from dull to colourful – a green land above a grey and silver sea.

At 12.10 the male appears round the headland and I follow him east. My body becomes alive, adrenalin surges into muscles, my back tingles and I become a hunter again. Those senses which our ancient ancestors relied on for their survival are beginning to sharpen, earning me a living too. My eyes narrow in alertness at every movement and I promptly lose the male amongst the rocks below Kirkabister! Suitably humbled, I walk east, aware of my improved sense of smell, the characteristic scent of otter lie-ups and spraints separated with precision from the delicate aroma of seaweed and grazing sheep.

Red-throated divers croak in celebration of their arrival on the voe from the hill loch, and when others join them to fish, they wail loudly, laying their outstretched necks on the water in aggressive posture, beaks held wide, red throat contrasting with smooth grey head. As still more divers join them, their croaking increases in intensity, and the cacophony of wails reaches a climax when with necks and bodies held erect, and head bent down at an acute angle, the combatants rise out of the water and run across the surface side by side, spray flying. When fatigue causes their levitation to cease they drop back and dive, rejoining their respective mates in silence.

I walk on round the big bay, and find a large group of male eiders

forcing their attentions on one lone female. They swim around her in excitement, breeding plumage immaculate, their bellies black, backs white, breasts flushed with pink, startling green patches on their napes, and black crown stripe angled down like a guardsman's peaked cap. The female swims in the tangle, a drab brown, looking as if she is trying to appear oblivious of the attention she is receiving, and the chaos she leaves in her wake. The suitors chase and peck each other, manoeuvring in order to be the one closest to her, and as they pass across her bows they throw their heads back and purr a delightful and seductive 'coo'.

Searching the cliff tops round Burraness I find the signs of only one otter

and grow tense at the lack of activity, and anxious by day's end at the lack of signs or sightings of my female. Despite the rich variety of wildlife I feel an emptiness without her, a tangible sense of loss. I feel I have no hope, and head back towards Dals Burn in gathering gloom. My spirits rise temporarily as I see an otter near the Burn Bank Holt, but on closing rapidly, I discover it is the male again. I follow him west towards evening, creeping along under the bank, but a curlew and I become aware of each other simultaneously and after a moment of inspection and doubt, the curlew flies off, screeching in alarm. Thus alerted, a great black-backed gull moans its warning and oystercatchers pipe off loudly down the shore. Its confidence broken, the male otter hides briefly, then slips off into the dusk towards the sandy bar of the South Ayre of Cunnister. This reminder of the difficulty of my challenge I could have done without, but the beauty of my location is undeniable. I walk home to the barely perceptible trilling skylarks as they sing in the darkening sky.

We watch Liverpool win the European Cup and I immediately feel a little better.

✳ ✳ ✳

I am hidden on the beach at Burraness by 3.30 a.m. Sea and sky are the dullest grey, there is a fine drizzle but the scene is one of utter tranquillity. The seals sleep, and I imagine all the otters do too. There are no fresh tracks on the beach, but I wait optimistically.

Eventually the day begins to stir and far out in the sound a busy flock of gulls, terns and auks, feed on a 'ball' of sand-eels, driven from below by predatory fish. It is not long before the activity attracts several gannets, and they plunge into the mêlée taking their own share of the harvest before the depleted shoal breaks up.

Thus amused, I find time passes quickly, and it is just after 6 a.m. when I notice a ripple along the far shore of the wee lochan behind me. I swivel the camera away from the beach and crouch lower, the otter having climbed out of the water. It sniffs at a clump of rush, spraints, then kicks the vegetation around and has a good roll. After a minute or so, it runs along the shore towards me and repeats the process at two more prominent tufts, kicking turf and mud vigorously, just like a dog. It looks like a youngish animal, its coat rather pale and features rounded, certainly not my female. Slipping back into the water, it dives, and the line of bubbles leads directly to my hiding place in the peat bank. Surfacing close to me, but unaware, it rises smoothly from the shallows, seemingly oblivious of the change from water to air. It drinks from the burn, follows it down the beach, spraints on a rock in the sand, then slips without hesitation into the sea. I watch it cross the bay towards the broch, but eventually lose it in the distant tangle. I wait in hiding for my female for three more hours, but she fails to appear. I circle the headland and head back towards Kirkabister, spotting what looks like a large, dark female in the Bay of Braewick, but which promptly disappears. It was not my lady.

Rounding Hivdigan Headland, I disturb a large herd of seals in their slumbers, and they scramble into the sea in unison, snorting and splashing and treading water as they peer inquisitively at me, necks stretched, nostrils flared, eyes white-rimmed with fear. They relax, but the whole herd decide to follow noisily just behind me, and I have to take refuge inland until they decide I have gone. When I regain the coast all bar two have departed. They circle round each other as if in courtship, blowing bubbles and splashing the surface noisily with their flippers, sporting like bathers.

When I reach the stream that leads up to the Hill Holt I discover a fresh spraint, and the distinct track of an otter up through the sphagnum. My spirits rise, for this is in the heart of my female's territory. I search all day, finding more signs of fresh activity, and begin to be convinced she has survived and has returned here. I fail to find her, but am on the shore again before dawn.

❊ ❊ ❊

I walk east in the cold, shady light, chilled by a slight breeze, but all that ripples the surface is the ebbing tide, trickling through the rocks and tangle in its mysterious languid sinking.

In the Bay of Braewick I discover a recently fledged brood of ravens. They flutter chaotically about on inexperienced wings, with only partially grown primaries for support. They are jet black, echoing the shadows of departing night.

The sun rises, its light climbing down into the dark recesses of the cliffs; the permanence of the rocks such a contrast to the ephemeral nature of my otter. At the broch there is a spraint on one of the ancient stones, a sign of the present close to one of ages lost. Perhaps she has fooled me and is right here, right this moment, watching me from somewhere along this shore. Self-doubt tortures me, it tortures us all, but I have learnt to accept the failures of the task, as well as its wonders.

As I think about the reasons for failure a sense of determination sets in and optimism returns. If not today, then work for tomorrow; search thoroughly, work hard, walk hard, think hard. I return to Kirkabister and start again. As if to prove that miracles are possible, a starling mimics a song from the ruined cottage; the call is the liquid fluting of a golden oriole, learnt from some far off sunny land.

Creeping carefully east I scan the difficult angled slabs of rock carefully with binoculars, and discover an otter eating a fish on one of the far promontories. I scramble hurriedly but carefully closer, and breathless, slowly raise my binoculars as it chews. The fish is a lump sucker, the otter without doubt my female; there is no way I could forget her whiskery features and the scar from the crab bite still shows on her nose. I am so thrilled I can hardly contain my enthusiasm, and I crawl ever closer, the noise of my movements masked by the rattle of the rising tide. Washed by the waves, she backs up the rock towards me, and completes her meal just five feet away.

OVERLEAF LEFT
. . . she yawns, whiskers vibrating, water dripping from her lower jaw . . .

RIGHT
. . . great carpets of yellow dandelions and pink campion – they glow in the summer sun . . .

Once finished, she slips into the water and immediately sees me. Alarmed at first, she hides under a barnacle encrusted rock, but watches me from there. I wonder if moments of recognition pass between us, for instead of fleeing she swims around my prone form, 'snuffing' calmly, then climbs out of the water to my left and walks round me. I dare not look for fear of frightening her, but she almost steps over my outstretched legs. I wonder if she will sink her teeth into them! Walking cautiously to my right, she stands two feet away, looking at me, for what reason I don't know, then slides into the rock pool and lies there sleepily. She yawns, whiskers vibrating, teeth gleaming white, mouth a striking pink, water dripping from her lower jaw. She lies there for a few moments, eyes closed, then opens them to watch an oystercatcher feeding on a nearby rock. Another flies up the shore to join the first but on landing becomes aware of us both. There is no alarm call but the sharp wing beats of take-off convince the otter that danger is close by and she slides out of the rock pool, slipping below the waves, leaving no ripple to give away our secret.

She swims quickly east up the coast, climbs gingerly out, and curls up on rounded pebbles just below the ditch crossing. She sleeps for a while, then grooms. A hovering Arctic tern catches a sand eel and offers it to its mate, which sits on a nearby rock. The otter watches the delicate aerial manoeuvre, finishes her groom, then heads on round the coast to the Headland Holt. She appears to want to come ashore here, but perhaps she catches my scent, for I lose her, and curse, for there is still a remote chance her cubs have survived, and that she will lead me to them.

I circle back and despite the dull weather, stay until dark. Little stirs the sea and sky; there is an air of dull repetition, of monotonous searching. Grey grass nods alongside grey sea.

✷ ✷ ✷

Turnstones twitter as they fly ahead of me down the shore; I have disturbed their nocturnal slumbers. It is another soft, grey dawn, the headland calm, slumbering. As I crawl into my hiding place by the beach three Arctic skuas zoom just over my head, their wild cry echoing off the nearby cliffs of Sandwich. The fulmar colony stirs and white wings circle silently in the half light. One of the skuas cannot resist a dive at the gull roost on the beach. They rise in a crescendo of calls, then all subside and there is peace again.

At tide's edge, green and brown seaweeds drape the rocks in graceful curves. A languid swell rolls sleepily along the beach, the silence between each wave almost tangible, the pauses hypnotic, as if the next wave will never arrive. They count the hours away.

As the tide starts to flow the movement becomes more urgent. Suddenly a chorus of curlew spring up in alarm and an otter appears at the far edge of the bay. It swims out from the rocks to the south of the broch, a series of shallow dives taking it far from the shore. It starts to fish. I walk east round the beach, but the otter is gone by the time I reach the Ruined Cottage

Holt. There is fresh otter activity here and rock pipits rush around insect-catching, the flies attracted to the holt by the smell of spraint.

The air is suddenly filled with the aggressive chatter of Arctic terns and I rush across the moor from the ruin, suspecting a predator. In the marshy top of Burraness lies a mixed colony of Arctic terns, Arctic skuas and common gulls. All have risen in alarm. They stoop at a fast moving predator in the sedge, and I suspect an otter. Though an otter's prey is almost always fish, they will occasionally eat rabbits and fulmars, even adult terns, caught at night perhaps? Surprisingly otters will not eat birds' eggs, but if this chaos is caused by an otter I fail to see it.

The Arctic tern's local name is 'tirrick', a name which mimics perfectly the harsh but still attractive call. They are a delight to watch and as they hover gracefully above me, translucent white against the blue sky, I think it no wonder that the locals love the tern, the swallow of the north, herald of their Shetland summer.

In mid afternoon another explosion of alarm occurs just over the brow of the hill and I rush to catch the culprit as the terns screech in defiance and plunge at the ground. Then I see it, a tiercel peregrine, crouched over a tern, plucking the feathers from its dying breast. The peregrine is immediately aware of me, and staring defiantly for a moment, carries off his prey up over the Hill of Burraness. He is stooped on angrily by a cloud of terns. The Arctic skuas take advantage of the confusion, chasing and harrying some of the remaining terns in an attempt to rob them of their fish. This display of gymnastic aerobatics is impressive, and despite their piratical nature, I can't help admiring the grace and beauty of the determined skua. After a long chase, the excitement subsides, and peace reigns over the incubating birds.

I leave to film the flowers that line the shores and streams of Yell: great carpets of yellow dandelions, golden marsh marigolds, white daisies, blue violets, pink campion – they glow in the summer sun.

✸ ✸ ✸

The weather remains bright, and I walk all morning in shirt-sleeves, failing to find an otter until lunchtime, when I discover my female on a reef to the east of Dals Burn. She sleeps, yet she gives life to the whole shore. She rests on an isolated pinnacle of rock, barnacle encrusted, festooned with bladder wrack. She is curled up right in the confined space, her tail under her head, with chin resting on paws, paws resting on tail – a furry pillow. She has caught her daily requirement of fish in only an hour or two, and like most predators, can spend much of her day in indolent slumber.

I crawl across the lichen-covered rocks, then lie in the weed hidden from both wind and otter. The sun is warm, and I sleep too, waking as the rising tide wets my legs and chest. The otter still sleeps, so I shuffle forward to a drier spot, close to her sleeping form. She looks at me briefly, yawns, then sleeps again. I lie there, relaxed and happy.

The tide rises further, until she appears to lie sleeping on the water; then she is gone, leaving behind a vague longing. I stare at the boulder for a time, feeling her presence there, but slowly the conviction evaporates, until I am sure she has gone. There is a sad emptiness and I rise from hiding.

* * *

Cloud returns overnight so today, instead of the camera, I take the children. Their enthusiasm is infectious and they rush ahead, thrilled at each discovery of print or spraint. We creep up the shore to the east, and their excitement reminds me of my early days with the otters, when every clue caused a surge of adrenalin. Their delight is a reminder of mine, suppressed sometimes by familiarity and frequent failure, but they also bring home to me the privilege and uniqueness of the experience.

The tide is rising and we see the male, fishing distantly off Dals Burn Headland. We walk on and find the female too. Once again she is without cubs, and I reluctantly accept she must definitely have lost them and has yet to produce another litter. However, the sight of her fishing just offshore is enjoyed by us all, and the children can barely stay still in their excitement. She heads quickly towards the male in the west, but we are unable to keep up. Reluctantly we back off, but I shall return in August, spirits high, hoping to find her with cubs.

CHAPTER 7

Midsummer madness

IT IS August 14th, and good to be back amongst this wild, hostile, but beautiful landscape. I head for Burraness in the middle of the night. It is 2.30 a.m., but there is just enough light to see where to put my feet, for this is the land of the 'simmer dim'. My presence is noticed despite the darkness. I feel a thousand unseen eyes staring at my back, a spine-chilling experience. I spin round nervously but see only the dim form of sleeping sheep. I am tempted to hide, feeling more secure when out of sight. There are no croft lights for comfort now, all are abed except this tormented soul who walks the night.

It is still dark as I reach my hiding place on Burraness beach, but the black sky soon changes to deepest blue, and a thin sliver of yellow along the north east horizon begins to glow orange, then suffuses the whole sky red. Our supreme celestial star climbs rapidly above the far island of Unst, throwing a broad red carpet across the sea, the rich colour accentuated by being superimposed on waves of grey. The bar of light appears complete at first, but where it meets the shore the reflection is broken by the swell, the gentle lapping of each successive wave accentuated by the parallel bars of bright red light. There is something timeless in the swell, but I become slowly aware of the sun drawing away from my world, up into the morning sky.

There is an almost sacred stillness, like that experienced in a cloistered cathedral, and at first glance the coast appears lifeless. Then sounds of dawn show that to be untrue, the tapestry so rich as to be three dimensional. There is the delicate thin seeping of rock pipits searching the kelp, the ratchet-like calls of red-throated divers, the rushing of fulmars' wings as they sweep past in the updraught. The distant wailing of seals drifts across the sound from Hascosay and I imagine their toothy aggression, with flipper held in appeasement, as they contest a resting place but avoid full scale confrontation.

It is very bright by 7 a.m., the sea a dazzling golden yellow, but in the water shimmer I notice a distinctive ripple, and my female appears, swimming along the sea's patterned surface. She climbs ashore by the rocks, carrying a large butterfish, whose head and tail swing side by side as she pads up the sandy beach towards me. She hesitates when she sees me, her step faltering slightly, but then she hurries on, up the stream and into the wee lochan behind me. A line of bubbles betray her route to the far shore but I never see her surface; she disappears. Perhaps this fish-carrying indicates cubs, but where? Her secretive behaviour is not going to assist my search. I wait two hours for her to reappear but in vain.

I walk the beach and find fresh tracks, etched sharply on the sand; they lead away from the Ruined Cottage Holt. I wait here too, watching the ringed plover catch corophium; the locals have a delightful name for this appealing dumpy bird, the 'Piree Sandy Loo'.

I search for otters all day, finding only a wet footprint on rock; the sense of being watched is acute. Perhaps the big tides make fishing easy, and the otters' daily requirements can be caught during the night? Perhaps I am too obvious in the bright sunshine, perhaps the otter feels vulnerable, or I am just too confident, taking too much for granted and due to familiarity, growing careless. I walk on, fearful that the coast is one of memories, as if all those experiences were a dream. I cannot get to grips with my otter now. She let me share her secrets just once, but no more; the privilege has been withdrawn.

The water turns black and drops of spray jump up to catch the light as it leaves the island. Then the sun is gone, the day is gone, the full moon rises. I watch the clouds drift over its pitted surface, wishing man had not reached such a remote goal. I listen for the whistle of otter cubs on the beach, then move west with the moon, following the sun's path across the blue black sky. No whistles penetrate the sombre silence. At daybreak the moon sets with the darkness in the west.

* * *

At 4 a.m. a whimbrel greets me with its fluty whistle, flying out from the hill and over the ruffled voe; curlews only manage a croaked alarm. I wait six hours in my hiding place by the beach, then growing impatient, search the beach to discover an otter walked past only half an hour before I arrived! My notebook shows evidence of extensive nocturnal wanderings:

fresh tracks at Ruined Cottage Holt, at least three otters and tail drags in sand, possible cubs, into holt at half ebb, about 4 a.m. – tracks of two otters walking west on beach, one just after high water but before rain, one at same place but after rain – little sign of activity at Hill Holt run, or along ditch – fresh spraint at lochan exit, but no tracks on sand – guess washed away by high tide – lots of spraint at Ruined Cottage Holt and Stack Holt – Headland Holt looks deserted – remains of lump sucker on Hivdigan Headland, freshly eaten – no otter sightings.

The suggestion of young cubs from the tracks in the sand excites my attention, and I circle back towards the beach from Headland Holt; on the way I find an otter by the ditch mouth and am torn between watching it or returning to the beach. The otter brings a sea scorpion ashore and when I creep closer and discover it is my female, the decision is made for me. When she has finished eating, she walks up the boulders towards me and drinks from the trickle of water which runs from the ditch mouth. Thirst satisfied, she cuts diagonally across the beach towards Kirkabister and I am amused to watch her broad behind and tail waggling back and forth as she tiptoes from boulder to boulder. She heads east along the very edge of the bay, the water only inches deep, but dense with bladder wrack; her movement is masked by the swell and she swims almost invisible.

On reaching the stream that leads down from Hill Holt she sneaks

ashore and checks the spraint spot on the bank. I am hoping intently yet again that she is leading me to cubs, but she just leaves her mark and heads down to Kirkabister. On the rocky promontory below the farm wet paw marks linger where she passed; I leave her and hurriedly return to the beach at Burraness.

My hunch has been right but my timing wrong: I should have come straight to the beach instead of following my female, for the tracks of a mother and two cubs lead from the lochan into the flooding tide – I missed them by half an hour. I continue my search, but high water arrives with no success, and I grow tired of the incessant wind. I have tried to live like the otters, by the rhythm of the moon and the tides, but I cannot sustain the disruption to my own rhythm for more than a few days, and night gives way once again to sleep.

✳ ✳ ✳

I am on the shore again by 4 a.m. but even this early hour seems too late on such a bright morning, for there is a sensation of emptiness along the shore. It is strange how one's senses analyse a situation and how accurate those sensitive indications are. It is also strange and amusing how wrong they can sometimes be, for within moments of my deciding I have no hope, the male swims ashore by Dals Burn, frightens an oystercatcher as he does so, then eats the eel pout he has brought ashore. The meal completed, he drinks from the burn, fishes unsuccessfully in the bay, and then heads for the shore at the big rocks beyond the fence. He seems surprisingly reluctant to come ashore here, and eventually climbs out some ten yards to the east. As I creep towards him, my female appears in the big rocks and I realise why he was hesitant, for she is aggressive and approaches the grooming male with head lowered, giving him the otter's version of a growl, a high pitched repetitive 'chitter'. He backs off and settles some three feet away whilst she takes over his chosen spot, though not without much sniffing and cautious circling. Both groom peacefully and rest for a while, then the click of a lens change alarms my female – she seems

BELOW
. . . the land of the 'simmer dim'

OPPOSITE
. . . her tracks lead away from the Ruined Cottage Holt . . .

inordinately highly strung today – and she slips into the water and commences fishing.

The male becomes restless, and he swims offshore to fish alongside her. He is half-hearted in his hunting, and spends most of his time watching her, either lying on the surface when she eats a fish, or ducking his head under the surface to watch her when she dives. He approaches several times, but she ignores him and moves away, eventually swimming rapidly towards Kirkabister; male otter and I follow.

Walking happily into the sun, I bump into another otter, which swims past me, oblivious. I do not know which one it is, and puzzle over this as it continues to chug away from me, along the shore to Kirkabister. A huge bank of cloud builds across the sky, obliterating the sun, and the wind increases from the south west, but I walk on round Burraness and find another otter near the Stack Holt. The wind funnels my scent down the cliff, so the otter disappears quickly, but not before it is identified as an adult male, probably from the next territory to the north. I double back to the ditch, then cross the headland to the beach. The sky is overcast, rain threatens; I am glad for the shelter of my hiding place, reached through a mêlée of sheep, who were using it for shelter before me.

As soon as the sheep have cleared my field of view to the east, I see an otter and two cubs swimming round the bay to the Ruined Cottage Holt. Rushing out of hiding, sheep scattering, I run, crouching, along the top of the beach, using the low bank behind me to break my outline. I fear losing the otter family in the weed and rocks, so stop, breathless, to watch. Mother and cubs climb out on to a rock, then restless, swim about amongst the tide-washed weed and boulders. They appear and disappear in the swell, but I suddenly realise there are too many heads, not one too many, but three! As they all climb out on to a reef I realise there are two families of cubs, and two females, one a very dark brown, the other a rather large, pale, old-looking individual. They seem quite amicable, for I hear only the slightest whickering before they settle on the reef just a yard apart. Their cubs swim around playfully together before joining their respective mothers but neither family settles for long and they swim off in opposite directions, the dark female towards the broch, the old lady across the bay. I follow this group and they eventually reach the cliffs below North Sandwick, disappearing into a cave behind a jagged stack. I cannot follow, for the tide is rising, and with the rain falling steadily now, I head for home. However, for a day which started as a 'no hoper' ten otters is not too bad! Despite the rain driving into my face, I walk back happy and optimistic: with two sets of cubs I surely cannot fail.

* * *

Frustration – so much to film but the weather awful, the wind unrelenting, rain driven fiercely across the voe, grass held flat against the ground, quivering. The far shore is obliterated by low cloud and salt laden spray. Shetland at its worst, one of the windiest places in Britain; sometimes it

seems like the windiest place in the world. So dominant is the wind that any day without it is reckoned to be a fine day, regardless of what else the weather is doing! Bobby tells me an amusing saying about Shetland weather: 'Bad? We receive three months bad weather and nine months of winter!' I am told that Shetland holds the record for one of the highest wind speeds in Britain; the anemometer reached 202 m.p.h., whereupon it blew away! I chuckle at the thought and retreat indoors to await an improvement.

✳ ✳ ✳

Tranquil dawn, tense calm, the wind holds its breath, the cloud lies quietly on the sky. As I reach Kirkabister I try to tiptoe across the dew, so profound is the silence. Approaching the shore, I hear the crunching of fish and in the half light I can just make out the form of a feeding otter. I sense it is the male but cannot be sure; I try to walk away in a whisper.

Reaching Burraness beach I find the footprints and spraints of an otter family. They are remarkably fresh, the pad marks rising out of the tide edge, the dew knocked off the grass. They are comparatively easy to track, even in the pre-dawn light, and I retrace my steps along the ditch, back along the shore to Hill Holt. Here their tracks come out of the water so close to the tide edge that they must have gone into the holt a mere ten minutes ago; we must have passed on the way! It is an eerie sensation to know you have been so close to wild animals without realising it.

The next track is disturbing; a human foot has trodden in the mud at the ditch edge. I fear human disturbance more than anything else. It is difficult

OVERLEAF LEFT
. . . she is aggressive as he approaches . . .

ABOVE RIGHT
. . . she drags ashore a huge female lump sucker . . .

BELOW RIGHT
. . . then leaves the rest for the cubs . . .

enough to anticipate the movements of undisturbed otters, let alone those that have been frightened, and I have no way of judging what the erratic homo sapiens will do. I follow the ditch to the beach, worried at this new development.

I walk until high water at 5 p.m. and though there are several fresh signs of otters I fail to see a single one. The confidence takes a beating for I know there are ten otters in the area. Perhaps they become totally nocturnal in this holiday season, when so many folk walk the shore, disturbing the otters daytime isolation? True or false, all I can do is persevere.

When I return to the beach, the male is fishing across the bay. I creep round in the falling light, watch him walk up the sand, then swim across the lochan. He makes surprising speed as he follows the ditch to Basta Voe, but I manage to run along about thirty yards behind, his arched back bouncing along, silhouetted against the reflection of the evening sky. When he enters the water his sleek brown body appears black on the pale blue surface. He heads west, each dive punctuated by radiating rings of deepest blue, echoing the east's dark sky. Night has already reached Fetlar

and it engulfs us as we reach Kirkabister; I leave the otter where I found him before dawn.

* * *

Only three hours sleep, the weather no incentive to rise, having turned grey and wet whilst I rested, but John Busby is with me for a few days and such an incentive easily overcomes fatigue. We head for Burraness, the steady drizzle making his watercolour work a trifle tricky.

After three hours we find the dark female and her four month old cubs, working their way through the shallows to the south west of the broch. We follow close behind, enjoying this success after days of frustration. The cubs eventually settle on a flat ledge below the broch, and sheltered from the wind by the ancient walls, we crouch on the damp grass to watch their mother fishing. The cubs go to join her, attracting the attention of the nesting fulmars, who hang just above them in the strong wind and dip gracefully down, close to the fishing trio. They appear more inquisitive than aggressive and the otters show little response.

The female has immediate success and eats several butterfish, before dragging ashore a huge female lump sucker, much to the delight of the cubs, who race alongside her. She opens up the stomach and eats a little, then leaves the rest for the cubs, who scramble about on the fish and eat greedily. The tide is flooding, and with the chop from wind and current soaking the feeding cubs, one of them tries to drag the fish on to a higher ledge. Growing tired of the mighty effort, it has to let go, and the fish drops back into the sea with a splash. A watching great black-backed gull moves closer, anticipating a meal, and is eventually satisfied, for the cubs, satiated, rejoin their mother, who has worked south through the shallow, kelp-strewn reefs.

The family eventually climb ashore about a quarter of a mile south of the broch, on a ledge at the very base of the cliff, sheltered from the wind. We are able to lie on the wet grass some forty feet above them, and look straight down on their antics. There is a cave in the cliff at the back of the ledge, leading into a narrow geo, and mother and cubs amuse themselves, and us, by climbing in and out of the hole and rolling about on the bright green enteromorphal-lined rock pool. A wren takes an interest in these antics and rattles in annoyance from just above the cave. The female hears this and peering out of the hole, neck twisted round, looks directly up at the wren. Large carnivore stares at diminutive insectivore for a moment, then the otter retreats back into the hole and the wren flies to the top of the cliff, scolding us instead.

The female appears to grow tired of the cubs' restless romping and heads back up the coast to the north, eventually swimming up a deep and narrow geo, just to the south of the broch. They climb carefully over the slippery green boulders into a dank, dark, dripping crack in the cliff. Though we can barely see what they are up to, they make what looks like a far from snug nest in the storm washed kelp at the back of the cave. The cubs suckle for a while, or at least try, then they all grow motionless, and we assume they have fallen asleep. We suddenly realise it is 6 p.m.; wet and cold, we retreat to the comfort of the fireside.

✳ ✳ ✳

The weather shows no improvement at dawn but we risk another soaking and head for Burraness, finding two otters hunting just to the south west of the broch. We are exposed to the full force of the strong wind and the otters remain unidentified in the choppy sea. John's hands chill quickly in the wind and drizzle, so drawing proves difficult, though he perseveres for a few hours. We eventually lose the otters in the rough water and head home.

In the evening the wind suddenly dies, the atmosphere uncannily calm in the damp, overcast condition. I find the male fishing near Kirkabister, then he climbs ashore and sleeps peacefully, oblivious of the midges. I hope his mate is indoors, suckling a litter of cubs. They will be blind and helpless at birth, but after nine weeks or so they will be out of doors. I shall return in October.

On the ferry home John and I have an enjoyable evening discussing our prospects with David Spence, the 'amphibious botanist'. He is one of the most dedicated of regular visitors and earned his name in his attempt to map the Shetland flora. Seeing an island in the middle of a loch, and being more than eager to check its vegetation, he had no boat, so stripped off and swam to it! You have to be keen to do that in Shetland, even in the summer.

CHAPTER 8

Success at last

THE STORM is unrelenting, the sea a chaos of wave and spume, accentuated at regular intervals by three towering waves of angry water, exceptional swells which are driven on to us by the fierce northerly gale. The ship shudders as it plunges into one of these troughs and meets the wall of water full on the bows. Spray flies from stem to stern and as we reach the crest the propellors rise clear of the water and scream with wasted energy. We falter in our progress, then plunge on into a seemingly endless succession of big seas. Progress is slow, but the great waves charge on like chariots, to batter the far coast of Scotland, unaffected by the impact of thousands of tons of ship. The creations of man are as nothing when faced by the true forces of the elements and the only evidence of our passing is a wash of turquoise and white in an otherwise dark grey sea. Where this wash meets the swell the water explodes in cascades, lifted high in the air and driven south by the gale. Erratic lines of spume wisp away towards the vague horizon. Though it is daytime it is still dark. Lowering grey clouds obliterate the sun, rising behind the depression that brings us this wind from the Arctic; rain falls steadily.

The first sight of Shetland is Fitful Head, looming in the gloom, but no gulls fly to greet us, they are incapable of following the boat in the storm.

Kittiwakes are blown backwards but the graceful fulmar seems at home in the gale, sliding gracefully between the white-capped waves. There are more gannets now, heading effortlessly into the teeth of the gale, bound for the crowded cliffs of Noss. Bressay looms to the east, and we creep under the welcome protection of its cliffs. We arrive at Lerwick three hours late, then spend a further hour hanging by the bows, unable to winch the stern to the quay against the bitter wind. A tug comes to the rescue and I step ashore and shiver, for this is a far cry from the tropical savannahs of Brazil; I was working there just seven days ago and it was high summer – this feels distinctly autumnal.

There was a time when I would shudder at the thought of trying to look for otters in this climate, but I have learnt to be unconcerned at what the elements throw at me. The rain turns to sleet as I drive north, so I shelter indoors and chat to Bobby and Betty, whilst the wind batters away at the windows and walls. It is October 7th; winter seems close by.

✳ ✳ ✳

The tide is just beginning to flow when I reach Dals Burn at 8 a.m. Fifteen common seals are hauled out beyond the fence, sheltered from the strong northerly wind. It is cold and wintry, raw on the skin; the storm still rages, but the sky is brighter now, the cloud broken. There are no bird calls, no song, just two silent mallard, feeding in the kelp. The male otter fishes off the headland. There seems no surprise to see him there; it is as if neither of us had ever been away.

He catches a sea scorpion and eats it on the shore. Grey and common seals swim up and watch him, he turns and snuffs at them, completes his meal, then edges cautiously around the shore towards me, as if avoiding the seals, just offshore. I remind him of my scent and he hides briefly, then climbs out on to a rock and rests until washed off by the tide. He walks across to the burn mouth and drinks for three or four minutes, then returns to the rocks for a groom. One of the common seals drags itself ashore and watches him closely, and sensing its presence he looks up briefly, then curls up and falls asleep. The seal, losing interest, returns to the sea and swims to Kirkabister; I follow.

In the fields at the farm, lapwing fly up, black and white against green and grey, then two redshank, all white wing bars and fluty calls. Trying to get my breath in the gale, I imitate them, but they only hesitate for a moment. Tiny goldcrests shelter under the cliff with fieldfare and redwing, suggesting they are all travellers from Scandinavia, blown off course by the storm.

I walk on, finding signs of otter activity below the Hill Holt and along the ditch across Burraness. I follow this into the teeth of the wind, over purple moor grass, quivering to its blast. The wee lochan is whipped into a foam, white against the dark peaty water. Along its banks the grass and sedge is flattened and tunnelled by much otter activity; I suspect the playful antics of cubs. Reaching the beach, there are nocturnal footprints, but the unsullied sands of summer have been stripped off by the autumn gales, and the beach is now composed of boulders. The wind is cold and strong, making my eyes water, and with the sea so rough on these exposed shores I consider my chances of seeing otters are slim. I retrace my steps, buffeted by the gale, clothes pushing and tugging as I lean into this hidden force.

On reaching Dals Burn a flock of curlew and golden plover drift away downwind and settle near the shore. I walk down the burn, and am suddenly confronted by an otter, running towards me over the grassy headland. I lie flat, and unaware of me, the otter spraints on the edge of the stream, enabling me to identify it as my female. She sniffs the sprainting point, I assume to check who else has passed this way, then slithers into the burn. She reappears on the bank further up stream, short-cutting a meander, then plunges back in and I fail to see her again. However I know she has continued into the hills, for the sheep watch her intently as she travels up through the heather. She must be running, as their eye-line changes rapidly to the north. I wonder at her haste and follow quickly, flushing snipe from the wild iris at my feet; they zigzag silently away.

I find frequent signs of otters up the burn, flattened banks, tunnels in the iris, holes and spraints, and follow her trail up through the grass and heather – merlin country this, but they will have headed south to the sun with their meadow pipit meals. I check all the holes on the hill but the fresh signs of otters have died out and there are no active holts here. I have lost the otters' tracks too, so return to the beach and find a fresh pad mark at the burn mouth – whose? Did she continue her journey over the hill to North Sandwick, or, not for the first time, double back on me unobserved? Whilst puzzling, I see an otter bring a fish ashore beyond the sleeping seals and the problem is solved, pad marks and otter must be the male. Simple, until I notice the male sleeping close to where I left him three hours ago. I rush up the shore, scattering the seals, but the unidentified otter is gone. I search for some time, but see only three distant mergansers, far to the west of Dals Burn. The male otter has disappeared too, but the Burn Bank Holt is well used; perhaps he hides inside? A light drizzle has started and darkness falls early.

❊ ❊ ❊

It has rained heavily overnight and the moors of peat squelch underfoot. There are new arrivals from some distant land, three whooper swans on the hill loch at dawn, having crossed the ocean from Iceland or Scandinavia, flying through the black night on broad white wings.

The wind has moderated, the shore silent but for the tinkle of the burn. A wren flits in front of me, keeping a yard between us. It does not call, as if not wishing to break the silence; all I hear is the whirr of its tiny wings. Purple sandpipers fly up the shore, sharing a soft murmur of calls. A great black-backed gull watches suspiciously on a rock and I wonder if its presence indicates that an otter has passed by. As I creep towards him I see a brown movement in the rocks and my adrenalin surges, but a long beak appears, a feeding curlew. The gull calls in alarm and the curlew's neck stretches to see the danger. I am still, and it continues to feed. I move closer, admiring its mottled back and extraordinary long bill with which it probes the weedy pools. Then the gull flies off, silent, but the manner of its departing speaks volumes. The curlew springs up, uttering one note of insult, and two turnstones rattle a line of abuse as they depart. Rounding the headland, I see an otter swimming away from me, and wonder if the gull's alarm was responsible for its departure.

I am discovered, and a whole chain of events follows. Mallard take off and land near the sleeping seals, most of which rush quickly into the water. More curlew jump up and several rock pipits seep around me in alarm. A snipe springs out of the seaweed and a starling squeals from the top of the bank. The otter looks over its shoulder and disappears behind some rocks. I retreat from the onslaught.

As I cross Burraness the roar from the breakers on the beach increases, and reaching the crest of the rise, the bay and lochan come into view. There are signs of mother and cubs here, three spraints together, just an hour or two old, so I climb the hill to watch. Standing in splendid isolation on the edge of this wild scene, it suddenly comes over me how lucky I am, looking down from my heavenly perch on autumn's sea and sky, grass turned yellow ochre by the salt-laden spray. Fulmars glide by – I wish I could fly.

Walking the windy cliff top, seeing no otters, I wonder how I achieved success before. In retrospect it seemed so simple, but then I remember the weeks of walking, the many days of failure and despair and I begin to doubt whether I can subject myself to that again. Feeling daunted and not too determined I lie down in order to rest my binoculars on a knoll, so holding them still in the wind. Scanning the wide bay in hope rather than belief, I see an otter snuffing around on the grass above Ruined Cottage Holt. I rush down on to the beach, cursing the boulders that impede my progress. The otter is heading fast towards the broch, its head splashing into the waves. I run, breathless, when suddenly the otter is running in front of me up to the broch, then behind the tall north wall. I creep round the broch, not knowing where I might see the otter next, then see it in a pool below the cliff, fishing; I can take a breather.

Watching the otter root about in the kelp from close by, I am surprised to see that it is my female, some way out of her normal territory. She catches a butterfish, crosses several reefs between rock pools, then heads along the shore through the waves; perhaps she will lead me to cubs this time, for I am convinced she has them: her teats are obviously distended as she runs across rocks between the pools. She swims south, unhurried and after half a mile cuts inshore into a shady geo. I peer over the cliff edge, then duck, for she is climbing up the cliff towards me! I retreat a few yards and settle, just as she reaches the top and walks from deep shadow into bright sunshine. She looks over her shoulder at me, is unconcerned, and investigates the rabbit burrows on the cliff top. Her head pops up after a

OPPOSITE
*. . . the holt lies below,
named after the old fence . . .*

114

while, watching me again, then she continues her journey along the cliff top at a trot, her arched back bouncing up and down, silhouetted against the afternoon sky. She disappears over a rise and I hesitate, afraid to rush forward for fear of frightening her, but anxious not to lose her. I wait for two tense minutes, then creep over the rise, and she is gone.

Even more doubtful of what to do next, not sure where she will pop up, if at all, I climb carefully over an old fence and look over the cliff, then notice some spraint on a ledge near the top, back off hurriedly, and hide. She appears immediately near the cliff top where I stood, and sniffs around the grass, checking out my fresh footprints – the tables are turned! She spraints on one, and I wonder whether this is a gesture of trust or intended as an insult! She walks to the edge of the cliff, climbs down on to the ledge, then into a large hole; it is another holt. I suddenly realise how remarkable is this even spacing of the holts and lie ups, for this new discovery is equidistant between Ruined Cottage Holt and Stack Holt. This one lies below the old fence, so that becomes its name: the Old Fence Holt.

I wait half an hour, then she climbs out of the hole, without cubs, and climbs down the cliff to continue her journey south. Disappointed, but wondering what the long visit meant, I have to follow her, and anticipating a visit to the Stack Holt, run ahead and settle just across from the entrance. She duly appears, swims into the geo, then climbs the steep cliff with ease, sprainting and glancing at me on the way. Reaching the top, she enters one of the holes, only briefly this time, then spraints twice more on the stack top before walking along the ridge, flushing a fulmar from its ledge on the way. She looks so fine as she climbs down, rugged cliffs around her, the sea ruffled by wind and tide – Fetlar and Hascosay distant, but bathed in sunshine. A beautiful animal, at home in her world, going about her business, undisturbed, free from the pressure of man. I watch in admiration as she enters the sea, diving deep through the kelp in fluid grace. I do not see her surface.

I wait by the Headland Holt, anticipating her appearance, but without success. I watch the restless water, sea pounding rock, spray turned gold by the setting sun. Tomorrow I shall commence my search right here.

✳ ✳ ✳

The tide is ebbing by breakfast time, and in the big bay beyond Kirkabister, the seals are selecting their low tide haul out. It is a fascinating process, for they have to forecast the weather. They try one place, decide the wind will return to northerly and haul out nearer the farm. They are restless here, and finally predict the wind will indeed shift to the east (which probably means rain I think), and move round to the beach near the Headland Holt. In the lee of the cliff where they lie the sea is black, but the merest ripple from the wind turns it silver. Otter and cub will do the same, but at present all that ripples silver are the seals. I detour well inland to avoid disturbing their basking, but though they cannot see me they thrash off the rocks into the bay; my scent was enough – shelter is not the only advantage of an offshore wind.

Finding fresh spraint at the Headland Holt, I wait some distance away, thinking the cubs must be inside. After nearly two hours a sudden movement alerts me and I am ready for action but of all things, a hedgehog hoves into view! It splashes past me through the marsh, and away on some purposeful mission.

Another hour passes, and I reflect that the cubs might only be outside for four hours each day, and that could easily be at night. However, all I can do is keep watching and waiting, and at exactly midday my perseverance is rewarded; I spot a mother and two cubs in the kelp on the far shore of the bay. I walk carefully around towards them, having plenty of time, for they appear to be settled in the weed on the shore, the female grooming peacefully. When I have crept close enough I realise it is indeed my female – she has produced cubs again. I am thrilled at this good fortune, but there is little surprise for it seemed inevitable that she would have cubs again – sometime – and that I would eventually find them. They look to be three to three and a half months old, so, as I suspected at the time, she was indeed hiding cubs from me in August, though they would have been too young to be brought out of the holt.

The cubs are certainly energetic now, romping about in the bladder wrack, and when their mother walks along the top of the shore and investigates an old disused holt in the bank, they climb in and out, slither down the grassy slope, falling on each other, then roll playfully. One climbs back into the holt, and appearing out of the top, finds mother and cub gone, for they are already some way along the beach. It squeaks anxiously, then sees them and runs along to catch up. Once they are together, their mother leads them along the shore towards Kirkabister, investigating the high tide mark like beachcombers. When they reach the burn that leads down from Hill Holt the cubs climb the bank and disappear up the gulley, whilst their mother swims off towards Kirkabister and starts to fish.

I stay with the cubs, or try to, for at first I am unable to see them. Most of the burn runs underground, but where it is on the surface, I discover the furrow in the sphagnum where they passed. Creeping along the bank, I listen intently and then become aware of their progress by the splashing from below. I back off, and eventually a little head pops up through a hole

and they climb out, rolling around with apparent joy on the lush burnside grass. One is slightly larger than the other and when their coats are dry they certainly look like male and female. Resting for a moment they suddenly seem to realise that their mother is not present and rush up and down the hill along the stream, in and out of holes, calling loudly. I try to keep tabs on them without being seen. It is a sort of hide and seek – I am looking for them and they are looking for their mother. Growing tired of this, they curl up on a fern-lined shelf by the burn and, settling down quickly, fall asleep.

I wait nearby, watching my female catch three small fish before she approaches the burn mouth, where she spraints. To my surprise she does not climb up the hill to join the cubs, but swims off round the bay towards the Headland Holt, and I am struck how misleading this would appear if I had not already found the cubs. I follow her, and she passes four cormorants, who chase each other whenever one of their party makes a catch. I lose my female round Hivdigan Headland and when I leave them at 4 p.m., the cubs are still bundled up at the stream edge – fast asleep. The wind has swung to the east and it has already started to rain – the seals were right in their morning weather forecast.

✳ ✳ ✳

Half-light, dawn a broad strip of pink across the eastern horizon, the gentle curve of the islands still without detail in the golden dawn. So still is it that the wings of crows can be heard leaving their roost. I jump as a snipe flushes out of the dying iris. To the east, a curlew leaves the shore and calls with fluid music, echoing from the cliffs across the calm water.

I see movement ahead, but closer inspection reveals four mergansers, perhaps those that hunted the spot yesterday. One calls a single note, an explosive guttural rattle, relieving the silence with sudden surprise. They fish, their crests thrust skyward as they search head down in the shallows.

Beyond them, a ripple leads out from the rocks, half a mile away, and swims my way. It is a silhouette, but the head is rectangular, flatter than that of a seal, and smaller; certainly an otter, but which one? I lie on the edge of the cliff, dew seeping through my clothes. The otter passes below me, I think it is my female. Perhaps she has left the cubs in the same place as yesterday, but that would be too easy! I check the spot anyway, and there is nothing. A spraint betrays their passing, but a cobweb across their track suggests they departed during the night. I return to where I last saw their mother, but she is gone too. I scan the seaweed shore. I see no brown fur breathing quietly in the tangle – nothing disturbs the mirror calm.

I walk west in the direction I think she headed but five hours later I find her to the east, close to the Stack Holt. She fishes on the wide kelp ledge to the south, catching a large octopus, flushed red with fear, and drags it over one of the rock stacks. Reaching a ledge below the Stack Holt, she starts to 'disarm' the octopus, a lengthy business. As she does so I notice a small fluffy tail sticking out of the holt; I have found the cubs again.

After eating a little, their mother tries to drag the octopus up the cliff, but finds it difficult, for the numerous tentacles drag between her legs, tripping her up. Eventually reaching the top of the stack, she delivers the meal, retreating rapidly back down the cliff, and well she might, for there is fierce competition between the cubs. A tug-of-war develops, amusing to me, but obviously in earnest for the cubs, for there are squeals of disagreement as big brother, inside the holt, tries to drag the octopus in, whilst little sister, attached to the other end, tries to drag it out. Eventually she is dragged in, but her behind still sticks out of the holt, and jerks back and forth with the effort. Using the edges of the hole as a lever, she manages to drag octopus and brother out, and the contest continues on the precipitous slope. I hold my breath, fearing another disaster, for if one should suddenly let go or a tentacle pull off, one or other would tumble to its death. However, they remain remarkably secure, spreading their weight and digging into the grass with their claws, and eventually call a truce, chewing either end of the now dusty and unpalatable looking octopus. There is an occasional angry whicker and snatch, but both appear fairly replete when their mother appears with a large wrasse.

She eats a little, then her son grabs the bulk of the fish, whilst her daughter finishes the octopus. Their mother has to flatten herself to squeeze into the holt, and the little female soon follows, but by the time her brother has completed the wrasse he is decidedly rotund and has to wriggle back and forth to enter the holt. Peace reinstated at last, I return to Kirkabister, meeting a local schoolteacher and his wife and child as they collect driftwood. With the otter family fast asleep, I welcome the company, and we walk back, enjoying the beauty of the islands and sharing thoughts on the benefits of life by the sea; I regret never asking their names.

❊ ❊ ❊

Clouds have been gathering steadily since mid morning and now conspire to produce a short, sharp squall. I shelter as best I can under the bank below the Hill Holt, and the worst of the weather goes over my head. By 2 p.m. the sleet has eased to a drizzle. Having wiped the rain off my binoculars, I spot an otter below Kirkabister, heading my way. As it passes my crouching form it hesitates slightly, smelling human scent, but whichever otter it is seems largely unconcerned and swims on towards Burraness. I follow a discreet distance behind, but the wind funnels my scent down the cliff and the otter keeps on turning to check where I am, before swimming on at high speed. Each time it watches me I have to remain stationary, then run in order to keep in contact; the speed an otter is capable of sustaining is a constant surprise.

After passing Headland Holt the otter suddenly hesitates just short of Hivdigan Headland and scanning the rocks I discover why: my female and her cubs are there, eating a fish. The otter I had been following goes on round the headland by sea, for the normal short cut that all otters seem to use is blocked by my family, and an otter with cubs is always to be avoided, as the male discovered last year! I am unable to stop my scent reaching the family, and they hide in the weedy, rock scattered shallows. The little female cub becomes separated and squeaks loudly, and her mother, growing anxious, starts to search with her son. Whilst they are distracted I shuffle down the cliff edge towards them, not only to hide my silhouette but to seek shelter from yet another squall. Soaked anyway, I watch as mother and son search ever closer to the lost cub, then finally seeing each other they rush together. The greeting is a touching moment, mother and cub nuzzling each other's faces, briefly, but with obvious affection.

Reunited, the family turns seawards and curl up for a groom and play on a wave washed rock. Their romp looks like 'king of the castle', for as soon as one climbs to the top of the furry pile, another wriggles out from underneath and clambers up, perhaps to avoid the storm-driven waves. The contest is playful, but pointless, for they are wet already, the rain falling relentlessly from a heavy sky. There is no apparent chance of a break, so I head for home, leaving the family to their games. The rain falls long into the night.

❊ ❊ ❊

The weather has changed, dawn is bright, the wind is light. The fields below Kirkabister are busy with new arrivals, but sadly my appearance disturbs them. Four greylag geese are the first to flee, followed by redshank, lapwing and golden plover, creating a kaleidoscope of black and white, red and gold. The grass is a lush green in the low sun, and several mushrooms linger on along the cliff top; they will make a tasty breakfast. Out in the voe a pair of herring gulls bob on the waves, their long calls a welcome echo of summer days.

Walking round Burraness, back and forth, I search hard for four hours, but failing to spot an otter, head home for a late breakfast. Returning to Basta Voe in mid morning with Sue and the children, we are driving round the head of the voe, where the burn runs out, when Peter says excitedly that he has seen a seal. Knowing this is no place for a seal, I stop the car, and there is his seal, an otter! just 25 yards away in the burn. I congratulate him on his sharpness of eye, for the otter is half hidden amongst boulders. Not daring to move, we watch the otter as it suddenly rushes out into a pool, scattering the sea trout that have ventured upstream on the night's tide. Having hoped for two years to film this rarely sighted behaviour, I creep silently out of the blind side of the car and manage to extract camera and tripod without alarming the otter.

I slither down the bank to the stream edge, the otter distracted by the fish it cannot catch. It moves upstream to another pool, keeping low over the gravel, then entering the water, noses along as flat as possible in the water, before suddenly rushing forward in great supple bounds, plunging torpedo fashion into the head of the pool. The trout panic away, their bow waves clearly visible in the shallow water. They dive beneath the undercut banks – the otter follows, nosing about for several minutes in these deeper spots, but finally climbs out, empty jawed. Frustrated, it walks amongst the boulder strewn shallows, turning rocks over with its front paws, or occasionally nosing them aside with its sensitive, whisker-lined muzzle – no wonder their noses are frequently scarred. By way of consolation, the otter finds and chomps minuscule bootlace-thin eels, but cannot resist the occasional unsuccessful foray back into the nearby pools. The otter works its way downstream now, back towards the sea, eventually climbing out and crossing a grassy headland, close to where the burn turns the sea a peaty brown. It disappears over the hill – I follow, leaving Sue to drive the children home.

Topping the rise, I see the otter some way below me and to the west, fishing offshore. Walking carefully towards it, I notice two cubs in the rocks, one of which lies asleep, a half-eaten sea scorpion close by, the mouth of which is nearly as large as the cub's face. As I approach, the female swims ashore with a large fish, much to the delight of the cubs, who wake and rush up to snatch it from her. The female returns to the sea, and the cubs begin a determined tug-of-war, the rope consisting of a golden coloured wrasse. Each cub has a firm hold on either end, and they brace themselves with hind feet against the rocks, backs arched in muscular effort. Each whickers in annoyance as they manoeuvre sideways to seek advantage, but then they subside as either tiredness or hunger takes over,

and they agree to eat their respective ends of the fish. There is an occasional flare-up of hostilities as one tries to catch the other unawares and snatch the fish, but they are both alert and tenacious and the head and tail of the fish finally part company, one of the cubs falling backwards into a pool as the tension is suddenly released. Completing their respective halves the cubs curl up together as if they had never disagreed about anything in their lives. They fall asleep in the sun. Walking on back to Burraness several hours of searching follows, until I find lots of fresh spraint at the Headland Holt. I retreat very gently, imagining the family inside the holt, their sensitive whiskers touching the edges of their peaty cavern, feeling the vibrations of my footfall. I wait for two hours within sight of the entrance, but perhaps I did not tread carefully enough, for no otters appear. Growing anxious at what I might be missing elsewhere I walk on, finding a half-eaten octopus on the kelp ledges near the Stack Holt, a lifeless witness to the otters' presence. There were no cubs here, for insufficient octopus has been eaten.

I search every nook and cranny to the beach, then back past the broch, right round to the Headland Holt but with little sign of activity. Unsure of what to do next I decide that the solution to my dilemma is to do nothing! Sitting quietly, my otter family appear out of the holt after half an hour, and climb calmly down and across the beach to the sea. The evening is calm, and we all share the pleasure of the fine weather, they rolling about in the weed as they groom, I sitting above them on the cliff top, looking out over the voe as the clouds of dusk gather across a pearly sky.

A heron flaps its deliberate way through the scene, to land in the rock pools where the ditch trickles into the bay. Chasing some frightened piltoch, it flaps its wings as it runs, and scares the seals, sleeping nearby. They splash into the water, which frightens the heron, and it takes off with loud squawks. The commotion falls heavily on the silence and my female is immediately alert, standing high on a rock to peer across the bay. She turns quickly, ushers the cubs into the sea, and they swim in tight formation off round Hivdigan Headland. I am sad to see her go, for this is the last time I shall see them until winter. Tomorrow I must travel south.

CHAPTER 9

Tracks in the snow

THE ALARM clock tolls and I slowly become aware of the wind and rain rattling the window panes. It is 5 a.m. and I wonder if I can afford to turn over and have a lie in, or whether for the sixth morning running I should try to find my elusive family of otters. It is still dark, but an improvement in conditions could make me regret my idleness; I have been caught before by changeable weather.

Breakfast eaten and flask of coffee prepared, I strengthen my resolve after five days of failure and walk out into the cold, grey dawn. It is February 16th, a sleet shower stings my face, and as I search the lonely Shetland shore, the wind makes my eyes water, tears from the cold adding to those of frustration. The sea is grey and choppy, but slightly paler to the south east, reflecting the skies more promising clarity. After an hour's walking the camera begins to gnaw into my shoulder. I rest briefly, then search for clues at the ditch crossing, and a fresh spraint rekindles my optimism; I walk on. After a couple of miles of depressingly empty weed and waves I reach the beach, and there in the sand are their tracks, the mother and two cubs; they lead right into the edge of the ebbing tide and I get the sensation that I am being watched. Then a great surge of elation; after six days searching I see them heading along the coast just beyond the Ruined Cottage Holt. New energy pumps into my tired limbs and I start a crouching run to try to close the gap without being seen. But there are two problems. The wind is blowing along the shore towards the otters and with it my scent. They are swimming away along the coast, so I must circle around them – fast. The biggest problem is the sloping shore, which means I cannot avoid showing my silhouette on the skyline, even by going inland. As expected the otters see me, though still 400 yards away. Now I am really up against it, but I run even further inland, beyond the ruined cottage, and try to overtake them; my scent blows down towards them and they are alarmed again. I try once more, and slither down a hollow to the shore. A pause for breath and there they are, not ten yards away, totally aware and watching me from under the seaweed!

I begin to accept that they have beaten me, but try circling once more before finally deciding that to alarm them too much may ruin my chances for the next time I find them. I argue that the angle of the light would not have been good if I had stalked beyond them, but feel angry and frustrated at the conditions that conspire against me. Watching the otters pass round the headland by the broch I feel not a little depressed – I have nothing to show for five gruelling hours, let alone the previous five days – I am alone and a failure.

As I walk south, my back sweats under my rucksack and the hard wind chills me, but finding fresh spraints at Headland Holt, I hide in the rocks under the cliff, seeking what shelter I can from the wind. The sky is more broken now, but a huge cumulo-nimbus towers up above the voe, and within an hour it is snowing. Soft white flakes fall on hard black rock, as they must have done when these rocks were part of a mountain chain, running from Scotland to Norway. In those far-off days, before the Ice Age, they must have reflected a deep, black cold, as they seem to now.

There are evening shadows by early afternoon but I wait on, determined but daunted, feeling powerless against the elements, not just wind and snow, but time and space. After days of defeat it's difficult not to give up, but I am so helpless that the easiest solution is to persevere; it is the only way to turn the days of slogging into success.

Once the decision to stay is made, it is easier to endure, and I become aware of the rare beauty of this wintry landscape, the scene a monochrome of black rocks, white land, grey sea. At least the otters' tracks will show up on the snow covered pasture, and as if in a gesture of encouragement for tomorrow, the weak sun peers shyly from below the confident clouds. However the otters do not appear and no doubt lie asleep in their holt, unaware of the snow storm.

As I head west the coast opens out to the falling sun, which bathes the shore in a golden glow. I walk hard to keep up with the light as it withdraws to the west; thus I manage to stay warm, despite the cold wind that follows me home.

✳ ✳ ✳

Winter has arrived with a vengeance overnight, and the snow has transformed the islands from brown and grey to black and white. The shape of the shore is etched with dark rock by the rise and fall of the tide. On the horizon towers a mountain of dark cloud, hiding the rising sun; above it the sky is luminous, below it the sea shimmers an icy white. Any otter tracks I find will be the work of the witching hours.

I sally forth, just as the sun begins to light the sky to the east, casting soft shadows over the pristine landscape. The snow lies right to the water's edge, for there is no swell on this calm morning, and even the tide seems paralysed in this frigid cold. Turnstone and ringed plover stand dejected on the lifeless shore, conserving their energy for a more promising time, but there is so much that enchants me in this spare, silent place that I move on softly so as not to break the spell.

My footsteps crunch in the snow, then grow quieter as the sun begins to soften the surface. Alongside me, lining the once dripping cliff, are great curtains of icicles, and Dals Burn only manages to flow under a thin filigree of star shaped patterns. Hastening flocks pass across the sky, and wild cries break the silence, barely audible at first, but growing louder as the wild chorus line wing their way south from behind the Hill of Burraness. They are whooper swans, white on white, passing Shetland by in favour of warmer climes. I imagine the otters would stay indoors, but they remain active in even the coldest weather, thanks to the warming influence of the Gulf Stream. There are still plenty of fish in the shallow waters, and the otter's dense fur protects it from the chill of air and water. But if they are active there is no sign of it at either Dals Burn or Kirkabister, and keen to keep warm, I walk briskly on to Burraness.

On reaching the ditch crossing I find the family's fresh tracks, etched deeply into the fresh snow, and follow them across the headland. On reaching the wee lochan I see clearly that they have done what I had hoped so much to film – they have been playing in the snow. Otters seem very fond of tobogganing, for several furrows lead down the nearby slopes and out on to the lochan, and where they lacked traction from gravity they apparently pushed themselves along on their bellies, legs flailing on either side like paddle steamers. Though I search Burraness thoroughly, there are few signs of otters in the snow, and disappointingly I fail to see a single one all day.

✳ ✳ ✳

The snow has retreated during the night, the salt laden spray has done its work, and the shore is dark once again. Missing the sun's warmth to make it glow yellow, the kelp has turned a dull green. It waves gently in the swell, as if it is sad at the passing of the seasons. Green lichens on the rocks have turned to gold and a few small red leaves still cling to the withered bushes on the shore, tattered remnants of summer, bearing witness to the tireless work of the wind. The marsh grass is blown dry, its colour a sickly pale ochre, the chlorophyll washed away by autumn rains. They are frost-covered now, held in the icy grip of winter.

OVERLEAF ABOVE LEFT
. . . transformed from brown and grey to black and white . . .

BELOW LEFT
. . . they have been playing in the snow . . .

RIGHT
. . . she peers through a gap in the rocks, unaware of my presence beyond . . .

On reaching the lochan of Burraness, I notice several isolated holes in the ice, and lines of bubbles trapped below; the otters have been here recently, and when I check the beach I realise just how recently. I have no time to hide, for the otters are just below me on the edge of the rocks. I go undetected and the mother and two cubs swim out into the bay – I cannot be sure which family it is yet, but retreat up the beach to hide and await developments.

No sooner have I settled than the female heads for the beach with a fish, followed eagerly by the cubs, who are now six months old, more than half the size of their mother, and evidently hungry. Feeling confident of not frightening them, I rush down the beach to the spot I think they will swim ashore, and though the female watches me as I approach, she only hesitates slightly before continuing to swim towards me; I realise that it must be my female.

The family surf ashore in the breakers and the female gives the smaller female cub the prey, a good sized plaice, which is alive! The fish flaps frantically on the sand, whilst the cub attempts to catch it, and though it finds this difficult, it eventually succeeds, just as the fish is about to make good its escape into the surf. Feeling more confident now, she lets it go again and chases it between sand and sea. Perhaps the female purposefully gives them live prey in order to sharpen their hunting instincts. The male cub is attracted by these antics and also tries to catch the fish, but little sister, eager not to lose her meal, grabs it and turns her back on him, chewing the head of the plaice as it wriggles in her front paws. My female grooms briefly nearby, then heads back offshore to fish, for she will have to keep up a constant supply of food for two hours or so, and do this twice every twenty-four hours.

The cubs are growing fast, and the male, unable to snatch any of the plaice from sister, heads offshore to join his mother. He is a capable swimmer now, and dives with ease, though the prey he is just learning to catch tends to be on the small side. When the female cub has completed the plaice, she too starts to fish, but both soon tire of this and head for the rocks below the lochan, followed by their mother.

Having a hunch they will walk across the sand to the lochan, I rush back up the beach and along below the bank, trying to reach my strategic hiding place before they do and I have hardly settled the camera when they walk through the rocks and up the beach towards me. They follow the trickle of freshwater, all three sprainting on a rock halfway up the beach, before drinking from the burn, then pass close by, totally ignoring my rather obvious silhouette. It is gratifying to be so accepted as part of the shore that I do not even warrant a glance, but it is a different story when they reach the lochan just behind me, for my scent is blowing inland and the female treads water for a moment as she nervously checks me out. Relaxing, the family nose around below the ice edge for a moment, looking unsuccessfully for eels perhaps, then return to the beach, sprainting on the grassy bank on the way. They walk unhurried, but purposefully, heading for the stacks below North Sandwick cliffs. They take a direct route, re-enter the sea and cut across the corner of the bay.

I hurry after them and manage to gain the cover of the rocks below the cliff without alarming them. They root around the tangle at the base of the stack, only their behinds and tails showing as they 'upend' to turn over boulders and sift the wrack for prey. The cubs follow their mother closely, learning from her example perhaps? She is ever watchful, checking around her for danger every few moments, but ignoring me.

On reaching a low reef, all three climb out to groom, and then roll in the wrack that festoons the barnacle-encrusted rocks. The cubs romp, climbing on each other, biting at ears and faces, then jump on mother, who, tiring of their boisterous behaviour, turns away and tries to rest. Discouraged, the cubs soon grow bored and slither into a rock pool. They seem to take a delight in disappearing under the weed, then appearing elsewhere, their heads comically covered in fronds of knotted wrack. As soon as one is discovered, the other rushes across the pool and tries to catch it. This game of tag goes on for several minutes, until the female cub hides by climbing out at the back of a rock, and her brother, unable to find her, slips up on to a flat boulder and circles round and round, trying to catch the tip of his tail. Both eventually return to their mother and settle down on a ledge, the cubs snuggling into her now dry and cosy fur.

I too rest, hidden close by in the rocks, savouring these moments of success. The female eventually wakes, and after a groom she peers through a gap in the rocks, unaware of my presence beyond. The family move off, not far however, for they clamber over the rocks and up a narrow gully into the cave under the cliff. I wait at its entrance for an hour, wary of being cut off by the rising tide, but as the otters fail to re-appear I head for home, striding through the remnants of the snow, full of well-being after a rare day of achievement.

Not for the first time, I wake to the noise of a gale battering the windows. The weather is quite horrible, but I venture forth towards Burraness under a threatening sky. The wind is so cold my eyes water, making binocular viewing almost impossible. My body is buffeted, sleet stings my face and as the fruitless searching continues I become increasingly humble; the force of the elements is difficult to defeat.

In mid-afternoon I find my female at Headland Holt, curled up in the grass just above the main entrance. She sleeps fitfully, looking around her nervously, and I fear the driftwood hunters of the past few days have made her anxious. She does not risk bringing out her cubs, but I wait until darkness drives me away.

✳ ✳ ✳

I wonder at her fearfulness, for two days go by without sighting her, or her cubs. Perhaps the slowly slipping tides have caused a change in daily schedule. She may even have become nocturnal, for she is so used to living life undisturbed that the appearance of human strangers is enough to drive her into old habits; the instincts for survival are not easily forgotten.

Whatever the reasons, I end this trip as I started it – in failure – but I shall return in May, undeterred, hoping for some fine weather.

CHAPTER 10

Fishing in the summer sun

P EACE, PERFECT peace; the sigh of wind through sedge, the soft rolling of sea on shore. I walk down the gentle slope towards the burn mouth, affection rising for the memories of success masking the realities of the moment. The drizzle deadens all activity and there is stillness, only the noisy silence of the elements. The spell is broken by the mournful cry of a golden plover, walking the dark moorland behind me, its cry a single note, blown away by the wind. Then there is nothing.

Now is the time of greatest tension, for my senses are out of tune, eyes and ears still dimmed by the clatter of civilisation. I lie still for a few minutes, soaking up the atmosphere, waiting for the otters to play their card – but nothing stirs. There is a deathly hush, as if the whole world is in suspension – watching – and waiting.

There is brown movement in the wrack – I move closer – and the movement is identified – rock pipits searching for insects on the tangled shore. I check the stream, as I have done so often before; there is fresh spraint and torn grass but the cobwebs are complete. I jump the burn and a small trout rushes upstream, its presence betrayed by the bow wave in the shallows. I pull on mittens to hide my white hands from the otter's gaze, but they are necessary for other reasons on this cold morning; the wind sweeps across the voe from Hascosay at nearly gale force – fingers and face chill quickly. Yesterday was even worse, the wind cutting down from the north, an icy blast from the Arctic. Whilst I was out on Burraness it snowed, just a few flakes at first, but then heavily for an hour or two. The salt-laden atmosphere ensured it did not settle for long, but it was not much of a greeting and quite unexpected for May 8th!

I did not see any otters yesterday but there are signs that my little cubs are still around, so I hope to do better today. It is 5 a.m. and high tide is at 7 a.m. – each day it will flood later, and I shall have an extra hour's good searching in these magic hours of dawn. I am optimistic for my future and bound on, full of energy. I find an otter in the bay by the ditch, but catch only tantalising glimpses in the troughs between the waves; almost as soon as it is found, it is lost. The drizzle becomes rain, the wind freshens to full gale force and my spirits are dampened – but not defeated.

I walk on and on round and round Burraness, seeing plenty of signs of mother and cubs, but not finding them. At the wee lochan I discover the cubs' nocturnal play pen, the soft rush at the water's edge, tousled and tunnelled by their vigorous activity.

The rain and wind ease at lunchtime and my spirits are temporarily lifted, but by 4 p.m. I have still not found the cubs. Ten hours of almost continuous brute labour and nothing to show for it. My step has lost its rhythm and I walk slack and stumbling, weary in defeat. As I rest by the broch the hot sweat on my back turns cold – I shiver.

Deciding I can take no more, I start for home, but choose to walk round the long way, just for one last try. As if such determination deserves reward, mother and cubs suddenly appear round a reef as I approach the Stack Holt. Whether they have come from there I do not know, but I am elated at finding them and new energy surges into fatigued limbs. I quickly scramble down the slope to escape from the skyline as mother and cubs swim towards me. I can recognise her, but not them, for in a few months they have grown so much they are nearly her size.

They swim close together, a cub either side of the female, who leads them by a foot or so, guiding their route round the coast. The sea is choppy, and they swim with heads held high to avoid their nostrils being swamped. This exposes their identifying features, and as they approach I see the male cub still has a distinct pink chin on his lower jaw, and a striking white patch on his chest. The female cub has no such marks, but shows contrast between the reddy brown upper part of her head, and the pale face and throat. Their mother looks much the same as ever, though in her efforts to secure the hungry pair enough food she has scraped the end of her nose raw whilst nosing under barnacle-encrusted boulders.

Moving north just offshore, they dive frequently, their mother always leading the way. But at over nine months old the cubs are evidently good swimmers and have learnt to hunt, for the female cub rises in the kelp with a small flatty, and undetected by the others, enjoys the meal, free of interference.

Her mother grows anxious at her disappearance, and stands atop a wave-washed rock 'whistling' loudly, her belly jerking with the effort of being heard. When the cub has finished its meal it too realises it has lost contact and whistles in slightly higher pitch, standing as tall as possible, raising a front foot as if in anxiety.

The cub finally spots her mother and rushes through the rock pools. Once reunited, they swim in unison around the headland into the Bay of Braewick. I lose the family momentarily, but find them again as they walk up over the large rounded boulders to a cave under the cliff. They walk carefully from rock to rock, trying not to slip on those that are covered with lush green enteromorpha. The male cub is shyer than sister or mother, and notices my silhouette on the cliff top. He stops and peers round the stack in disbelief, torn between fleeing to the sea or joining the family, who curl up and groom at the entrance to the cave. The male cub raises one foot, staring and 'snuffing' at me, then as I do not move, he relaxes and joins the others.

As a greeting he walks up and rubs his head on his mother's face, then stands on her back for a good look round and falls off when she moves. All three fidget around and groom, the pink toes of their webbed feet standing out strikingly in the gloom under the cliff. Within moments they regain the sea, fishing in the beds of weed between the reef. The female cub catches a sea scorpion and climbs on to a flat ledge to feed, only to grow aggressive and defensive when joined by her mother. She is not after her fish, for she carries a large fat, butterfish, and both chomp contentedly. The male cub joins them with a large flatty.

Satisfied with their meals all three swim quietly through the lush green kelp and clamber ashore on to a flat ledge below the stack, looked down on by fulmars, whose guttural croaking echoes out from numerous ledges round the bay. The otters climb over each other in constant motion, the female aware of me and slightly nervous, looking around anxiously, trying to ignore the cubs who try to draw her into play. Eventually she succumbs and becomes a part of their furry circle, each trying to rest their head on the rump of the next. The antics are complicated when the cubs attempt to suckle and root around, trying to force their way into their mother's curled up form. Having given up nursing months ago, she takes offence at this ridiculous behaviour and grabs one by the scruff, pulling it away, only to be assaulted by the next. They become a real 'ottery tangle' but the activity slowly subsides in sleep and they curl up nose to tail in a tight, cosy ball. Having run out of film I decide to leave them undisturbed and wend my way home; it will be a very buoyant walk, for the possibility of success has now become a reality. Two years of walking and waiting, of patience and perseverance seem worthwhile, for with a bit of luck, I will now complete the programme. Wildlife film-making brings many moments of failure and despair, but those of success and elation are intensely satisfying and this is one of them. Tired but happy, I sleep well.

* * *

Keen to follow success with success, I am out again at 4 a.m. but perhaps life is not meant to be like that, for by evening I have failed to see an otter. I am undeterred, for there seems to come a stage in a tidal cycle when otters lose interest in daytime activities and wait until nightfall to venture forth. Perhaps I am in that changeover period now, and will have to wait for them to start using the flood tide at dawn before I see them again.

As if to support my hypothesis, I find the female alone in Braewick Bay, fishing in evening's gorgeous warm light. She glows golden brown, contrasting with the clear blue sea. She swims slowly away from me out into the bay, pauses, gives me a glance, then dives into one of the sandy patches between the kelp. The evening sky is calm, the sea rippled only by the otter's dive. I follow her round the bay and rest motionless when she surfaces and chomps butterfish.

Eventually she moves south more purposefully, past Stack Holt and round Hivdigan Headland. I follow breathlessly, then, anticipating a visit to the Headland Holt, cut across the hill at a run and settle some thirty yards to the north of the holt. Within moments she appears round the rocky bluff below the holt, and looks cautiously around before climbing out of the sea and up the beach to the holt. She disappears behind a buttress in the cliff, then reappears out of one of the holes in the holt, looks around briefly, then disappears into another. Moments later a drier, fluffy, smaller head appears from one of the holes, then another; she has returned

OPPOSITE
. . . investigating the caves that lie amongst the jumble of smashed granite . . .

BELOW
. . . the cubs' calls penetrate even the thundering sea . . .

to her cubs. I hope they will now be taken out fishing, but evidently their mother intends to wait for nightfall, for there is no sign of her, and the cubs just sit in the entrance to the holt, gazing out over the bay.

The hills at the head of the voe grow purple, the shore lost in a haze. The silhouette of Kirkabister lies motionless, its reflection on the calm bay broken only by the surfacing of seals. As the sun sets behind the Hill of Burraness, the moorland glows a golden red, and the heat from our majestic star ripples the fiery band of light as it withdraws to the west. It grows narrower by degrees, then is extinguished, leaving the deepening blue sky of dusk.

With the sun gone, cold falls with night's shadow. Across the voe, a wink of lone light in a distant croft window increases the chill feeling of isolation. I am alone, but not lonely, for I am relaxed amongst so much familiarity. Each holt and headland is home of a sort, and I am happy to be here in such emptiness, free of intrusion from man. It is such a rich feeling I wish I could share this isolation, but by its nature this cannot be; the very presence of another human would destroy the sensation.

The light is gone, the otters sleep. I retreat silently, hiding my camera under a fish box to await the dawn.

* * *

I return at 2 a.m. It is dark, the sun still travelling the night, lighting the satanic shadows of Finland's pine forests. I collect the camera and check the beach for signs of nocturnal wanderings. The family's tracks are there all right, having crossed the headland and beach just after midnight. I hide in the bank, dozing in the half-light, waiting for the sun to complete its circumnavigation of other northern lands.

At 4.40 a.m. it casts its first shadows on the beach and I am able to track the faint outlines of the otters' pad marks along the beach. They follow the night's high tide and lead to the Ruined Cottage Holt, so I wait below the bank, a few yards away, convinced of the family's presence inside.

The hours pass by and I watch the graceful dipping of a black-headed gull as it floats in the freshening south easterly breeze, searching for food items in the gently rocking waves. Just along the beach a pair of Arctic terns stand preening. Other terns stand on the rocks, sheltered from the cold breeze by the low cliff, awaiting the return of their mates, who then hover gracefully by them to pass dainty morsels of stickleback as a gesture of courtship. Of the otters there is no sign, and growing restless, I walk up towards the noon sky, then sit aimless at the broch. The tide is wrong now; my body lacks sleep and optimism. I retrace my steps to the boat noost and, sheltered from the wind, enjoy hot coffee. The sun crosses high over my head, life disappearing with it. I fall asleep – the world turns.

Waking to the calls of gulls, I wonder at the commotion, and hurriedly, but slightly dazed, try to check the shore in the vicinity. I can only guess the gulls were calling at me, for of otters there is no sign. I check the beach, then circle back past the broch and Braewick Bay to the Headland Holt, but with no success. Returning to the beach, I am just approaching the Ruined Cottage Holt when the family walk nonchalantly down from the holt. Even though I have waited fourteen hours I cannot take advantage of this good fortune, for the wind is offshore, and try as I will, I cannot avoid making them cautious with my scent. I decide to retreat and have an early night. I leave them just below the broch, hiding in the wrack.

Dawn is heralded by cavernous, deep thunder as wind hurls water at the rocks. This turbulent place is at the mercy of immense waves, but it is just these powerful forces of erosion that are responsible for so much good otter habitat. The shoreline has been fractured, broken and fragmented, nowhere more so than on the far side of Burraness, open to the south-easterly gale.

As I approach Braewick I see one of the cubs in the waves and its calls penetrate even the thundering sea. It appears to be lost, for it swims back and forth, then rushes across the skerries, seeming oblivious of the difference between rock and water. It stands momentarily, raising one leg in characteristically anxious fashion, and sees its mother offshore, fishing in the big swells that sweep in from the ocean. I can see now that this cub is the little female, and she rushes seawards, the waves bouncing against her chest as she swims with head clear of the rough water. She lands on a reef just below the Old Fence Holt and her brother joins her; both stand anxiously looking out to sea.

Eventually their mother joins them and they cut across to the rocky headland, investigating the caves that lie amongst the jumble of smashed granite. They wander in and out, occasionally losing each other in the labyrinth, even to the extent of the little female cub heading offshore, squeaking loudly. She returns, and all gather on a sloping rock, only to discover me just above them. They take fright and rush across the rock into the foaming swell, but not wanting to cause a tragedy I back off and let them relax. They seem quite at home in these rough seas and I never cease to marvel at their agility and grace, even in these testing conditions.

OVERLEAF LEFT
. . . I can just make them out, grooming at the base of a crevice . . .

ABOVE RIGHT
. . . the family climb on to a shelf at the bottom of the cliff, and stretch . . .

BELOW RIGHT
. . . their mother tries to ignore their boisterous play . . .

They regain the rocks and groom for a while, before clambering into one of the caves. Perhaps they had been out for some time before I found them at 6 a.m., for they do not reappear and I assume they will sleep off the rest of the day. I check periodically throughout the day but draw a blank. I just sit and watch in awe of the wild, murderous, splendid power of the sea.

✳ ✳ ✳

The wind has abated by dawn, and the sun rises through a cloudless sky. If my hunch about tides is right, the family should be out around 7 a.m., but where? I head for Braewick in the hope they have spent their pre-dawn sleep in the Old Fence Holt, and as if by magic, I find the family curled up asleep on a flat reef in the northern corner of Braewick. The tide rises quickly and the latent swell from yesterday's storm contrives to wake the otters as it sweeps water on to them over the reef. They sleep fitfully, then wake reluctantly, and after spraining, head offshore to fish.

The male cub is the first to make a catch and brings the scorpion back to the reef, only to be approached by his sister. He snatches the fish away and climbs quickly to the top of the reef, to eat his meal in peace. Once this is completed he starts to play with his sister in the shallows, and as they roll about and duck each other, the swells of foam-flecked white water sweep them back and forth. Their antics are disrupted by their mother, who approaches with a butterfish. She is immediately chased, the cubs forging through the water, bow waves thrust from their chests as they pull alongside their mother and try to snatch the fish. The female porpoises through the surf, and in one smooth swift movement reaches the reef and runs to the top, the two cubs latched to her sides. There is a brief squabble and whickering, with heads snatching from side to side, then the little female cub is given the catch and she runs away to avoid competition.

Meagre meal completed, the three swim leisurely towards me as I lie on top of the cliff, then disappear under the overhang below. I have to circle round the bay to see what they are up to and can just make them out, grooming at the base of a crevice, which widens near the water to form a small cave. Mother and son investigate inside, but the female cub lies outside in the sunshine. Half an hour passes before mother and male cub paddle out into the bay. A few moments later I hear squeaks emanating from below – the little female has been left behind. I assume it sees its mother, for it suddenly appears like a brown torpedo, hurrying out into the bay in a series of shallow dives. Each time it surfaces air is trapped in its dense fur and when it dives its back is silvered as clusters of bubbles stream behind it.

The family group up, then climb on to a shelf at the bottom of the cliff and stretch, just a few feet below me. The cubs engage in their usual combination of grooming and playing, wrestling around on the ledge as they bite and push each other. Their mother tries to ignore their boisterous play, but as she is often underneath them she no doubt finds this difficult.

After several minutes the activity subsides and they circle into an ever-tightening tangle until they are curled up in a furry bundle, with just the odd bit of head and tail showing.

I have shared their enjoyment of this slumber for several minutes when I notice the male has appeared and is watching me from behind a nearby reef. He drifts along towards the sleeping family, lying flat and motionless on the surface, hind legs cocked sidewise in what I now recognise as a posture in preparation for flight. Perhaps he is torn between apprehension and curiosity, but when close to the others he makes a very splashy audible dive, as if deliberately alarming the mother and cubs. He disappears and the family, somewhat sleepily, slither off their ledge. The cubs hide behind a rock but their mother lies across the reef, looking at me with apparent lack of concern. After several moments of consideration, she dives into the crystal depths, swimming towards the cubs, her sleek brown body taking on a ghostly form. She propels herself with synchronous kicks, alternating rhythmically between front and back legs. Then she dives deep, waggling her hind quarters and tail like a large flipper, her legs held stiffly and spread wide to present as wide a propulsion unit to the water as possible. In this manner she disappears rapidly into the kelp, then appears some twenty yards further on, her rippled body pale brown under water. She surfaces with the cubs alongside a rock, then all three dive into the kelp and swim towards me.

The female cub surfaces first, and finding herself alone, dives again and swivels acrobatically in her own length by manoeuvring with her front paws. The three join underwater and they too use their front paws to manoeuvre, 'walking' over a ledge of rock, before surfacing just below the cliff. They clamber ashore very close to me, and though aware of me, seem more concerned at the whereabouts of the male. Satisfied he is not around they curl up to resume their sleep in the sun, and as it is nearly high water, I assume their hunting activity is over for the daylight hours. I leave them to sleep and retire silently.

✳ ✳ ✳

After two days of success I am finally convinced of the value of my hypothesis that there is a direct relationship between tide times and feeding times, so I head straight for the far shore of Burraness, but not hurriedly, for it is 6 a.m. and the otters are not due out until 8 a.m.! It is a relief to leave indecision behind, for when I reach Braewick the conviction that they will appear just here with the rising tide is so strong that I walk no further; I just sit and relax, a rare moment of peace of mind. The warming sun has discouraged the wind, and the sea ripples ever gentler below me.

How do I know the otters will appear here? Well, I have chosen the southern promontory of the bay, and this commands extensive views to the north. There is every chance the otters will not appear here of course, but it somehow feels right, and hunches sometimes pay off. I shall not lose

OVERLEAF ABOVE LEFT
. . . the conviction that they will appear at Braewick is strong . . .

BELOW LEFT
. . . then all three dive into the kelp . . .

RIGHT
. . . the male lump sucker falls easy prey even to young otters . . .

my nerve and look elsewhere until 8 a.m., so I pass the time watching rabbits feeding on the cliff edge, fulmars gliding below them, and in the bay several red-throated divers fishing. Time stands still for a while, moments memorised for ever by my mind; it is as if the whole coast is alive, but suspended – waiting – incomplete without the otters.

At exactly 8 a.m., as predicted, the otter family appear just twenty yards below me. There should be surprise, but I feel none, and just routinely analyse that they must have slept in the cave by the stack; simultaneously I manoeuvre into position for filming. They swim round to the south, keeping very close to the shore, then when they reach the large reef between Braewick and Stack Holt, clamber up and have a good weedy roll. I have come to call these 'Mediterranean Rocks', for they glow a sub-tropical white in the sun, covered as they are in barnacles.

Ablutions complete, the otters swim offshore into the tide and start to fish, whilst I scramble down the cliff and set up close to their grooming spot. All three soon have success, for they grow more proficient by the day, and the prolific summer season is with us. The poor old male lump sucker comes in for some stick, for he is conditioned to guard the eggs the female has laid, behaviour that gives them their other name, 'sea hen'. Being slow moving and bright red in this courting season, they fall easy prey even to young otters. The rocks soon look like a fishmonger's slab and though I am delighted to be so close to all this activity, I am amazed at how much the trio can eat.

Just when I think they must be satiated their mother appears with a large octopus, tentacles still exploring her face. She drags it ashore, lays it on the rocks and waits for one of the cubs to respond. The little female sees it first and though keen, is hesitant. She sniffs round for a moment, then throwing caution to the wind, tucks in to one of the tentacles. There is a sudden snort and whimper, for the octopus has attached itself to one of her front legs, and she runs backward over the rocks, vigorously shaking the paw to try to release the tenacious grip. She decides to attack, and standing on the octopus, bites the offending tentacle until it releases the grip. She then chomps hungrily at the meal, but not without the occasional manoeuvre to avoid the lunges of her brother, who tries to steal the catch.

After another hour of gastronomic greed, the fat family clamber up into the Stack Holt for what I assume will be a long sleep.

※ ※ ※

The glorious weather continues and I am ever more confident of capturing good film of the growing family. However, I hit a slight snag, for I am unable to find them! On Monday all I find is one strange otter in Braewick, who flees at the sight of me. Otters certainly are very decisive and when they go, they go. This one swims two to three hundred yards in just two dives and disappears round the northern headland.

On Tuesday afternoon I find my female alone, heading north past Stack Holt. I follow as best I can, but the wind is not in my favour and she draws ahead as she enters Braewick. Just as I am creeping up I hear awful screams and yelps from below; dashing up, I see my female in vicious combat with another. They wrestle together on a ledge by the stack, kicking, biting and spitting like two alley cats. The intruder retreats to a ledge half-way up the cliff and hides behind a rock, whimpering submissively. My female, honour satisfied, sniffs around the place the intruder must have been lying, as if trying to identify it, then spraints on the site of the battle. It is a mystery which otter it is, and why she should be so aggressive, for holts are for the communal use of all and to my knowledge my female's cubs are not close by. She heads south and I follow the intruder north, but am unable to recognise it, and then lose it just beyond the broch. I try to find my female again but fail, and walk home under the moon.

✻ ✻ ✻

On Tuesday 17th, I enlist the help of Bobby, for it is my last day and with conditions for underwater photography ideal at last, I will try to film

mother and cubs – if we can find them. We set off at dawn, travelling separate ways, but even circling independently around Burraness we both draw a blank and by 10 a.m. the wind and swell has risen and ruined our chances. Bobby heads home and I continue searching. Then, when I round Hivdigan Headland I can just make out Bobby crouched over by Kirkabister and know this means he has found them.

What they are doing so far from their normal 'patch' I do not know, but perhaps such wanderings are normal for a mature family. I rush round to Kirkabister but before I reach Bobby, the family have started back across the bay to where I came from. I double back to Hivdigan Headland, following them round until they settle to fish on the large kelp bed to the south of Stack Holt. There is no way I can swim in the tide with them here, so I content myself by filming their activities from the base of the cliff. They must have eaten well earlier, for each cub now plays with their catch. The little female has caught a small sea scorpion, and whilst catching and releasing it in a rock pool, raises her head up briefly to watch me, comically covered by single fronds of seaweed. She peers between them, then slithers out and releases the fish, but as it is now rather lifeless, nudges it in the manner of cat and mouse. Eliciting no response, she lies down, holds the fish between her paws, and like a child with a stick of seaside rock, chews and sucks the head.

Her brother swims in a pool nearby, playing with a male lump sucker that her mother has brought him. He rolls about on his back, holding the fish in his paws, then lets it swim off before diving down to catch it again. He plays like this for ages, a rather gruesome game, but one designed no doubt to sharpen his hunting instincts. At present life seems carefree, playing in a rock pool with the sun sparkling through the water, mother stretched out nearby, relaxed in the warmth.

There is joy here for me too, at one with the wilderness and all its marvels, where past, present and future merge into one. The fact that one is alive and living is enough, there is no need for nostalgia or hope.

Eventually, my female's instincts will tell her that it is time for her to breed again, and after a year of alert guidance from her, the cubs will drift away and establish a territory of their own – near or far – perhaps I shall never know. We do not even know whether female otters are able to breed every year, but if as they appear to be in Shetland, they are seasonal breeders, then my female will not be able to give birth to another set of cubs until next summer. It is a long wait for her, and a serious restriction on productivity, for she may only live for ten years or so. The oldest European otter recorded was thirteen, but that was in captivity, where the stresses of life are less extreme.

As the three swim to the north, I follow for a time, reluctant to see them go, but eventually the ferry calls, and I watch them swim gently north past the Stack Holt, through the narrow geo and away up the coast. I am unable to turn away until their ripples are no longer visible, for I shall miss them, and am sad at the passing of so many rich experiences, shared with them all. I may never see them again, but I hope I am wrong.

CHAPTER 11

Nostalgic return

'TEAS AND coffees will be served in the midships cafeteria.' The familiar tannoy announcement stirs me from my restless sleep. Reality and dream have become confused – voices in the dark, creaking beams, thump of waves, otters swimming, the rattle of plumbing, the lowing of cattle from the depths of the ship. I walk the decks to unfold the creases of the night. The grey mass of Bressay drifts across the ocean towards us; it is as if we lie at anchor as green fields and brown moorland entomb us in their peaty mass. Black rock skerries reach out towards us, holding out a hand in greeting, though a lighthouse on the most prominent reef suggests their intentions are less honourable. Dark cliffs close behind us and Shetland once more swallows me with its wild charm.

The drifting dream is broken by the ship's loud horn, celebrating our arrival. The grey rooftops of Lerwick angle down the hill to the very edge of the sea. It is a friendly looking capital, but the slates glisten in the northern wetness; the weather is unkind for July. One side of the ship is bitter cold, the north westerly wind scything along the steel; in contrast the sheltered side is just wet and grey.

Inland, heavy clouds hang veil-like over the moorland. Greys of sea and sky enhance the pastel greens of sheep pasture; rivulets of silver rush from the hills. There have been numerous days like this during my weeks with the otters and as fans of wind ruffle the surface with spasms of intensity I hurry in to shelter yet again.

This visit is an act of faith, for I come armed yet again with underwater camera, hoping for calm, clear sea conditions and a new family of young cubs for my female. In addition I hope to have one last try at aerial photography. I have tried twice before but the plane was too bumpy; calm, clear weather is rare in Shetland. On this trip more than any I need hope and faith, for optimism has often proved misguided and confidence is a fragile state of mind.

There is bad news to greet me too. Bobby tells me that outline planning permission has been granted by the Shetland Islands Council to turn Basta Voe into a maintenance base for the oil industry – my silent wilderness destroyed, the home of many generations of otters threatened and disrupted for just ten years' profit. No doubt the nation needs the oil, but maybe when it has run out, man will have learnt to protect those things of lasting value.

* * *

After a day's rain the weather dawns bright, though with the wind a fresh southerly it is too rough for flying. There is contrast to the rain and cloud, the sounds of sunshine; song of wheatear, skylark, lambs bleating, divers wailing. At first glance all appears as it was at Basta Voe, despite more than a year away, but on closer inspection there are sinister orange plastic markers on the far shore, and an oil rig looms like a predator over the green pasture of Hascosay – for how long may sheep safely graze? Despite these ominous threats there are still otters here, for even as I arrive, one fishes off the point. I am unable to recognise it offshore but it looks like a sub-adult. Anxious to find cubs, I leave it be and explore the coast towards Burraness. There is repetition in this search, the quest the same, day after day, week after week, but I must take as much trouble on these last days as I did on the first – the job requires perseverance, not patience.

I walk on past the ancient broch, trying to pay attention to every detail, trying again to become at one with this wild kingdom, adapt to its most subtle challenges. Reaching Braewick, I remember happily all those sunny days with mother and cubs last May. The prospect then was one of the loveliest of my lifetime; now they are gone the scene is barren and lifeless – that mere rock and water can vary so markedly in one's mind is, on reflection, marvellous in itself – at the time the sense of emptiness and failure is depressing. Walking round and round, searching the apparently empty shore, my peace of mind does not improve, but there always seems to be hope while the tide floods.

The wind increases, the sun retreats; I walk south past the broch for the third circuit and by the time I find the otters it is mid afternoon. A mother and two cubs – it is my female. It is thanks to happy memories that they are discovered, for they play on a ledge where John and I sketched and filmed her previous family, many months ago. The spot is easily missed; the ledge lies under an overhanging cliff and can only be seen by leaning over the edge. The female sits quietly, grooming by the little cave, but the cubs are engaged in the most boisterous bout of play I have ever seen, rolling together in a shallow pool on the ledge, attempting to bite each other's face and ears. There is the occasional squeal when one succeeds, then it breaks off, only to pounce cat like back on to the other, and roll back into the pool. They are so lithe and energetic, running after each other, springing in the air, plunging into the sea, leaping back out on to the ledge.

I have left the camera under a fish box near the ditch crossing, my added mobility enabling me to search more thoroughly – but how I regret that decision now! At first I decide the play will not last more than the usual few minutes, but the longer it goes on the worse I feel. In the end I run across Burraness and return breathless with the camera – but of course the otters are gone. I search long and hard but without success; I have blown it.

※ ※ ※

I am out by 4 a.m. It is a lovely, calm morning, quite bright despite the thick mist, the far side of the voe hidden, the sea smooth. The midges drive me mad – they are the only clouds on this marvellous morning.

Out in the voe a great northern diver wails its weird call as it floats somewhere between sea and sky – the elements are merged as one. Fulmars glide over the mirror, reflections following their every turn, taut wings skimming the surface. I walk east, finding mother and cubs offshore near the entrance to the Hill Holt. They must have completed their dawn feed, for they climb ashore as I approach, walk up the beach, and disappear into the burn. I follow them up the hill at a distance and they climb unhurriedly into the holt. I wait for a time but there is no stirring from within.

The mist clears and I scan the calm voe. There are seals and shags fishing, the occasional tystie, a family of eider. Just west of Kirkabister I watch an otter fishing, catching a butterfish on roughly one in every six dives. Then it brings a sea scorpion ashore, and judging by the otter's age and markings I decide it is the female cub from last year; what delight to see it alive and well. Whilst watching it feed a second otter appears, fishes, and drags a male lump sucker ashore; each otter appears oblivious of the other, even though they are brother and sister, for this second otter is undoubtedly the male cub. He still has his pink chin, and as he feeds I notice the distinct marking on his throat. I creep within five feet of him as he chews the lump sucker, waves splashing over us both as the wind freshens.

Once their meals are complete the two otters meet offshore, and though brought together by chance they renew old bonds in play, rolling offshore, then romping about in the seaweed. The female is bitten, and whimpers, bringing an end to the meeting, and she heads east to Burraness; I follow the male to the west. He fishes offshore, watched with interest by a common seal, who swims to where the otter has dived. The otter surfaces, then swivels round to find the seal just two feet behind it. It gets quite a fright and promptly plunges under the surface, to rise a few yards away, neck stretched, treading water, snorting with displeasure. The seal closes in again and the otter panics and heads rapidly for shore, followed closely by the seal. Whether it is play or aggression neither I nor the otter knows, but he flees out of the water just by me, with the seal close on his heels. He sits on the shore watching the seal and the seal stays a yard offshore, watching the otter. After ten minutes of this stalemate the seal loses interest and dives, then the otter gingerly re-enters the water and continues his journey to Dals Burn, but never swims more than two feet away from the safety of the shore.

Further down the coast on the Ayre of Cunnister, numerous common seals start to haul out on the sand bar. They seem to take delight in porpoising ashore, shuffling rapidly over the bar, then back into the sea with a great splash as they accelerate away into deeper water. The twenty or so that have settled lie in the sun, facing the water. Each moves down with the ebbing tide – in case of danger, escape is close at hand.

I return to Hill Holt, but my family are still apparently asleep inside. I wait until dusk but nothing stirs.

❊ ❊ ❊

I climb towards Hill Holt in the half light, dawn heralded by a glow from behind the hill, casting shadows over me and the coast below. The sky

BELOW
. . . greys of sea and sky enhance the pastel green of sheep pasture . . .

BELOW RIGHT
. . . the male cub still has his pink chin . . .

brightens from the eastern horizon, the white bog cotton glowing orange, each drop of dew magnifying the sun's rise. The light reaches across from the far shore of the voe and creeps down the hill towards me, eventually reaching the darkest recesses of the shore; even the black peat reflects the distant planet's power.

There is evidence of my family's nocturnal wanderings, and a subtle suggestion that they have returned here, dew missing from a cobweb by the holt's entrance. I retreat to wait for the afternoon tide. The day is clear, fresh and chilly, so I walk quickly to keep warm. On reaching the beach from the hill I notice an otter just against the shore, swimming towards me at 200 yards range. I hide in preparation for a close encounter but my scent is bound to be caught by whoever it is. As it swims past it falters, but looks around comparatively unconcerned; it is the previous year's female cub, but she has had an accident overnight, her right eye being completely bloodshot. Perhaps she had a fight, perhaps an over-boisterous game with her brother, or maybe my female attacked her in an attempt to drive her out of the territory? This sub-adult may well breed within a year and then there could be too much competition with her mother for food. Whatever the cause, she seems largely unconcerned at her blind eye and continues towards Kirkabister.

I follow for a time, but then detour to a phone, for the weather seems ideal for flying. I speak to Jim Dickson, who runs the Pollution Control Office at Sullom Voe and he kindly allows me a lift in their spotter plane on their daily check of the northern coasts. Dashing across on the ferry to the oil terminal at Sullom Voe, we are soon airborne and enjoying a spectacular view of Shetland from 3000 feet. The sky is blue, the scattered cumulus white, and we drift over them as the south coast of Yell passes far below, the shore flecked by the tide. It is so clear we can see far to the south over Mainland and to the north over Unst; we can just make out Muckle Flugga Lighthouse, the most northerly point in the British Isles.

Burraness appears from behind a cloud, my home for three years, a remote, lonely headland, jutting out into the sound between Yell and Unst. It is strange seeing the coast from up here, the distances different, perspectives changed, the significant rocks and headlands apparently insignificant. I feel detached, separated by space, but drawn to it by memories. As we circle, the land turns black and the surrounding sea shimmers in a shaft of sunlight. What a marvellous place – what magnificent coasts, one of the last great strongholds of otters in Europe. They have all they need here, peace and quiet, clean seas, wild shores and, above all, space. It is in our power to ensure they continue to have these simple requirements, inconceivable that we should remove them. Surely the otters are worth consideration? A reserve is perhaps an admission of defeat, for such protection seems inevitably to end with rules and restrictions – conservation's 'brick wall' mentality. Would it not be nice that the otters and their shore are open to all to share, a wilderness area for those who appreciate such subtle charms?

We complete our pollution checks and head back to the airstrip over Sullom Voe. There are flare stacks, huge storage tanks, jetties and super tankers – a most impressive complex and one which has been sited well to remain hidden from almost every angle in Shetland. But what a contrast to Basta Voe – as it is now.

I return to the Hill Holt by early afternoon and find my female and the two cubs lying asleep outside. The sun shines, the sea is calm, so I rush off to grab my diving gear, and Reg Hussey helps me along the shore with the heavy equipment. He will keep a weather eye on me as I swim, taking time off from the motel he runs. He has become interested in the project, for we have often seen otters from the windows of his dining room.

This opportunity to swim with the otters is as good as I could hope for, if only they will come down to the shore before the sun goes. At least we cannot miss them if they do and I use the time to get wet suit, bottle and miscellaneous equipment assembled for a stealthy plunge.

After what seems an interminable wait, the family appear and walk down the beach, unaware of us peering in anticipation from behind a bluff. Once they are in the tangle, I creep down the beach and slip into the cold, clear water. Still unseen, I start to snake towards the otters through the kelp. They swim offshore, and I can just make out their legs, paddling energetically. I swim offshore with them, only my mask and snorkel showing above the surface. They gain on me and I watch as they fish some twenty yards away, the swell much larger than it looks on land, the otters appearing and disappearing as the waves sweep over us. It is exciting to be out here with them, to see the world as they see it; the land distant, the ocean vast.

The female catches a large eel pout and rushes towards me with it, followed by the cubs. I back off slightly, and they pass me at remarkable speed, just three feet away. They rush ashore and I move into the bed of wrack to watch them feed. The normal positions are reversed, for I look at them in a similar hiding place from which they must have so often watched me.

Meal complete, they re-enter the sea and I sink below the surface, moving predator-like into their path. They pass just two feet in front of me, then as they swim out to sea I turn and follow, diving down with them as they start to fish. As they dive all three fold their front legs back and use just their hind quarters and tail, waggling them flipper-fashion. The female disappears into the kelp in a shower of bubbles, the cubs returning to the surface and searching for their mother from above. The cubs are about $3\frac{1}{2}$ months old and as yet seem only just capable of diving. They are silhouettes on the surface, for shafts of sunlight filter past them through the plankton, striking the sun-seeking beds of kelp as they wave in the ocean's swell. It is exhilarating, for I have at last joined them in their element – I am actually swimming with a family of wild otters, a final thrill in this totally absorbing experience.

Sadly, the experience is short-lived, for as the female rises out of the kelp

OVERLEAF ABOVE LEFT
. . . they greet by rubbing faces . . .

BELOW LEFT
. . . then play in the swell . . .

RIGHT
. . . the female holding him off with outstretched paw . . .

she notices me close by, and on surfacing she treads water and snuffs at me, her eyes popping in alarm. She dives again and I head towards the shore with the cubs, who stand on the edge, whistling for a moment, then retreat up the beach and up the hill to the holt. Fearful that I might disturb the family, I leave the water and hide with Reg, and he tells me that when I followed the cubs, the female hovered just above my leg with mouth held wide, looking as if she was about to attack. Maybe if she had sunk her teeth into me it would have been a final justice, repayment for all the times I have alarmed her; I would have considered it a final privilege! We retreat to dry off and warm up, elated at the brief success but relieved to see our female climb the beach and join the cubs. What a day – I have seen her domain from both sea and sky.

✳ ✳ ✳

The summer weather does not last, and for two days Shetland lies in a thick pall of damp fog. Sunday sees an improvement, and I seek out the otter family once again. It is still foggy, but I find the female in kelp beds close to Headland Holt. She is on her own and allows me very close. I like to think she has forgiven me, but in truth she almost certainly does not recognise me as the goggled diver. Perhaps she has no memory of such experiences; it would be nice to know.

Hunting the kelp beds, she plunges below the fronds, which thrash about as she searches beneath them, then she rises briefly again, comically behatted with a kelp frond. After five unsuccessful minutes she lies on a weedy reef, rolls on her back and with legs flailing in the air, rubs herself back and forth, wriggling about in apparent delight, for she closes her eyes as a human might when scratching their back. She seems too hurried to groom, and heads round the bay, climbing up to the Hill Holt; I suspect the cubs are there but I fail to see them.

Walking on to Kirkabister I can just make out an otter at Dals Burn, and though it is nearly half a mile away, it smells my scent and hides. I am impressed by this exceptional talent for survival, and circle round to investigate who it is. On reaching Dals Burn, the otter has caught an octopus and eats it near the Burn Bank Holt. It is last year's male cub, and though good at sensing danger he is inexperienced at octopus eating and becomes covered in ink. Just like his mother, who did the same more than two years ago, he snuffs, shakes his head, and tries to wipe the ink off with his paws; he even tries to clean his teeth with his claws. When satisfied, he sleeps for more than an hour, curled up by the tide edge.

The sun reveals itself by mid-afternoon and he wakes, soon to catch a flatty just off Dals Burn; he crouches in the wrack and chews the fish, eyes closed in the sun. He hears the camera shutter and swims to the headland, sinking and rising without a ripple, snatching air by putting just his nose above the surface, but only for a second or two. He looks like a piece of kelp, difficult to spot in the wind, but I see him hide in the reef off the point. He lies motionless under a frond of weed for nearly two hours. He certainly does have an impressive will to survive. I am glad that my 'conditioning' of the family has not made them less cautious.

Leaving him to relax, I retrace my steps towards Kirkabister and lie down on the beach to film the tide lapping through the bladder wrack. I have been there ten minutes when a barely perceptible 'presence' makes me look round, and there behind me, just a hundred yards away, is my female, searching the tide-washed wrack at the edge of the beach. It is as if this wild landscape is alert to her presence and my acute awareness of the moment to moment experience has put me in tune with the shore; I too can now tell when she is present, even when I cannot see her.

She is very relaxed, drifting towards me, so unhurried she yawns between dives. Passing close by, she glances at me and continues as if I was made of stone. She meets up with her son near the burn mouth. They greet

by rubbing faces, then play in the swell before climbing ashore on the reef and continuing to play, trying to bite each other like cubs, the female holding him off with outstretched paw. It is a moving experience to see such apparent affection.

The otters part to go their separate ways, and I follow my female to the east, hoping she will show me the cubs just one last time. As she swims on past Hill Holt and Headland Holt I begin to accept that I will not see them again. Maybe this is how it should be, spending my last evening with the otter who started the adventure. Memory stimulates nostalgia for the weeks that have passed, the moments of trust, her courtship, her first cubs, their loss, her new cubs' playful nature, the success and failure, the despair and elation; they are disturbingly familiar but gone before they can be grasped – three years have passed all too swiftly by.

Her world seems far away now, even though she still swims before me. I must leave whilst the memories are still fresh, but how is it that the end brings such regret? There should be relief and celebration, another assignment completed – instead there is sadness – a privilege ended. I watch her go until she is swallowed by the gathering darkness, then turn and, resting on the camera, gaze westwards, a last look at the coast that has seen so much of my life go by.

As for my otter, she retains that indefinable quality which appeals to the imagination; she is still shy and elusive, wild and free. Turning my back on the coast, I know I may never again see this otter that I have grown to love, may never again experience the trust she shared with me. Her life will continue unchanged – mine will never be quite the same again.

Technical notes

FOR THOSE with technical interest, the camera I used for filming otters was an Arriflex SR. With it were a range of lenses; a 10 mm wide angle, a 10 mm to 150 mm Angenieux zoom, and a Canon 300 mm/600 mm telephoto lens, giving 12 or 24 times magnification. I used a very heavy tripod head to counteract the wind, a Sachtler Panorama 7, mounted on wooden Arriflex legs. The camera is virtually silent when running, essential when close to the otters. As an extra precaution I painted camera, tripod and lenses green and brown.

Each magazine on the camera ran ten minutes; I always carried a spare, and even some extra film if I was feeling particularly optimistic. However, if I managed to shoot twenty minutes of film in a day I would reckon I had done very well. The normal ratio of film shot to film used in a wildlife programme is about ten to one.

When seen walking with the gear, I found I was often asked how much it weighed – my daily load was 46 lbs; it does not feel too bad at dawn, but by dusk it begins to seem very heavy! This equipment is fairly standard for all wildlife filming, and that used for otters has travelled the world with me, in search of new challenges.

* * *

To take the still photographs I used an ancient Pentax SIA, loaded with Kodachrome 64, then finding winding on difficult when close to the otters, promoted myself to a Pentax LX, with motor drive. The otters did not like the noise of this at first but they preferred the noise to the movement involved in trying to wind on the film by hand. I used a standard 50 mm lens, along with 28 mm wide angle and my 300/600 mm Canon filming lens adapted for stills. Bobby also uses a Pentax LX fitted with 400 mm Novoflex lenses, along with more standard focal lengths. Neither of us used a tripod, preferring to crawl on our bellies and rest the camera on a convenient rock.

* * *

But a word of warning, if I may. On most occasions otters are very shy animals, and may well suffer if continually harried and disturbed by careless approach. Make sure you are down wind and off the skyline, keeping movement to a minimum. The place I carried out my project is private land and though Shetlanders are most helpful, I did seek permission wherever I went. Otters are a protected animal, rare in so many places, so please respect their requirements for a quiet life, and respect Shetland, one of the otter's last strongholds.